T0318226

Using Virtual Worlds in Educational Settings

The building of communities outside of the traditional brick-and-mortar base of a school or university is at a significant point in time; virtual worlds bridge the gap between 2D web spaces online and 3D physical spaces of the classroom, providing teachers and students alike with opportunities to connect and collaborate in ways that were previously unimaginable. Providing insight into this new age of teaching, *Using Virtual Worlds in Educational Settings* presents a collection of practical, evidence-based ideas that illustrate the capacity for immersive virtual worlds to be integrated successfully in higher education and school settings.

Examining research and stories from more than 1,000 students and six faculty members who introduced virtual worlds into their teaching and learning, this book contains practical examples of how virtual worlds can be introduced and supported, as well as reflections from faculty and students about their response to virtual worlds. This research will help teachers understand how to approach such a fundamental shift in pedagogy, how to liberate themselves from teacher-focused instruction and how to help students to develop their skills through collaboration.

Outlining how and why virtual worlds could be the shift in pedagogy that teachers have been waiting for, *Using Virtual Worlds in Educational Settings* is an accessible, practical resource for educators to support their use of virtual worlds in teaching.

Lisa Jacka is a lecturer in the School of Education at Southern Cross University, Australia.

Using Virtual Worlds in Educational Settings

Making Learning Real

Lisa Jacka

Routledge

Taylor & Francis Group

LONDON AND NEW YORK

First published 2018 by Routledge

2 Park Square, Milton Park, Abingdon, Oxfordshire OX14 4RN
52 Vanderbilt Avenue, New York, NY 10017

Routledge is an imprint of the Taylor & Francis Group, an informa business

First issued in paperback 2020

British Library Cataloguing in Publication Data
A catalogue record for this book is available from the British Library

Library of Congress Cataloging in Publication Data
A catalog record for this book has been requested

ISBN: 978-1-138-30558-8 (hbk)
ISBN: 978-0-367-60725-8 (pbk)

Typeset in Times New Roman
by Wearset Ltd, Boldon, Tyne and Wear

Contents

List of images   vii
Acknowledgements   viii

Introduction   1

Innovation in education 1
Change and innovation 2
Barriers 3
What are virtual worlds? 5
Starting out with virtual worlds 7
Research 9
Conclusion 10
References 10

1 Virtual worlds   13

1.1 Introduction 13
1.2 Evolution 14
1.3 Affordances 17
1.4 Barriers 21
1.5 Potential 24
1.6 Conclusion 25
1.7 References 26

2 Disrupting norms   29

2.1 Introduction 29
2.2 A new culture of learning 30

2.3 Disruptive innovations 31

2.4 ITE can be the leaders 33

2.5 Virtual worlds in ITE 35

2.6 Virtual worlds in K-12 schools 38

2.7 Conclusion 39

2.8 References 40

3   Making learning real   45

3.1 Introduction 45

3.2 Truly twenty-first century visual arts 45

3.3 Exploring science and sustainability 54

3.4 Uncovering ideas about other cultures 59

3.5 Being an early childhood educator 69

3.6 Conclusion 73

3.7 References 74

4   Perspectives   75

4.1 Introduction 75

4.2 Barriers 75

4.3 What do ITE students think? 82

4.4 ITE faculty reflection 87

4.5 A critical lens 89

4.6 Conclusion 90

4.7 References 91

Conclusion   92

What we learnt 92

Recommendations 95

Where we are going 98

Conclusion 100

References 100

Index   101

Images

3.1   ITE visual arts students listen to a lecture on the
Interaction Island oval   48

3.2   ITE visual arts students listen to a lecture in one of the
lecture theatres on Interaction Island   49

3.3   ITE visual arts students create an exhibition space and
place artwork on the walls   50

3.4   The completed strawberry farm in which strawberries
could be grown with solar panels on the outside and
climate controlled on the inside   57

3.5   An avatar dressed as a World Food Program worker
stands amongst the simulated African village created by
one of the ITE students   61

3.6   A simulation of colonial Australia, including animals,
vegetables and a house created using prims and found
images   61

3.7   The Freedom Rides were represented with a simulation
of a swimming pool surrounded by images from the
event   62

3.8   Students were allocated space on a platform above the
island. This bird's eye view shows eight of the building
spaces   65

3.9   One of the builds addressed the theme of poverty
through the use of 3D buildings and 2D images   65

3.10   Three students perform a role-play as the Early
Childhood Director and two parents   71

Acknowledgements

This book brings together aspects of research that I conducted in the Teacher Education faculty where I have worked for many years now. I would not have been able to undertake this research without the generosity and support of my colleagues and our students. I would like to thank them for providing me with an environment in which these ideas could be explored and experimented with.

To my close family who have worked with me through the research and the culmination of this book, including my husband and our two children. Having school age children constantly reminds me of the importance of working with Initial Teacher Education students and K-12 teachers in order to encourage and support innovative educational practices.

Thank you to Art Education Australia for giving permission to reproduce part of my work previously published in Jacka, L. and Ellis, A. (2010) Virtual arts: Visual arts education in the virtual world of second life. *Australian Art Education, 33*(3), 125–139.

There have been many individuals who have helped me to keep my ideas alive and get them on to paper. They include colleagues from other institutions, professional educators and mentors. Thank you.

Introduction

Innovation in education

Education as a sector is generally considered to be conservative (Apple, 2014; Fullan, 1993; Vrasidas & Glass, 2005) and according to Goodman (2012) has become more conservative in the past twenty-five to thirty years. Both Apple (2014) and Goodman (2012) refer to the current state of education as being in a time of conservative restoration driven by test results and a society that is seeking validation that the money being put into schools is resulting in a measurable output from the students. The conservative environment in which schools are operating can stifle innovation; as Fullan (1993) suggested, when innovative change is attempted in conservative circumstances it 'results in defensiveness, superficiality or, at best, short-lived pockets of success' (p. 3). Even the implementation of innovation with the best intentions can have the opposite effect, as Hargreaves and Shirley (2012) highlighted with a study of 'charter schools' that showed a return to traditionalism. The forces of various stakeholders (market forces, parents' nostalgia and the schools that responded to both the market and the parents) put pressure on those seeking to provide alternatives to the traditional form of schooling and as such the capacity to change was hindered.

There are examples of innovation in education that demonstrate university faculty and K-12 teachers implementing new models of teaching and learning, often facilitated using innovative technology. Virtual worlds are one example, as are flipped classrooms, MOOCs, makerspaces, coding and digital-technology games. Introducing these technologies often results in a shift towards new pedagogical approaches, which brings with it a potential set of barriers as the faculty and teachers attempt to fit new ways of learning into an old structure (that of the Industrial Age classroom). Not only is there a requirement to include technologies that are, by nature, student centred, but learning approaches such as problem-based, inquiry-based and game-based learning have a significant role to play. Having the capacity, as a teacher, to change the way that you have been 'doing teaching' requires support. Initial Teacher Education (ITE) has a role to play in introducing faculty and teachers to new ways of teaching through modelling best practice and providing avenues for skill development.

Faculty and teachers who are making these shifts in their practice are also using technology to bridge the gap between what they know and what they can imagine by linking with other innovative educators through social networking tools such as Facebook, Yammer and Twitter, as well as guilds in games such as World of Warcraft. By using networked technology, educators can effect change more rapidly and on a larger scale, through support and collaboration. C. Christensen, Horn and Johnson (2011) optimistically express the potential for technology to effect educational change when they state:

> There is power in our communities to effect change. By disrupting the classroom as we now know it, we can break apart the fundamental barriers with which faculty, parents and students have struggled for so many years. These technologies and organizational innovations are not threats. They are exciting opportunities to make learning intrinsically motivating, to make teaching professionally rewarding, and to transform our schools from being economic and political liabilities to sources of solutions and strength.
>
> (C. Christensen et al., 2011, Conclusion, para. 21)

The building of communities outside of the traditional bricks-and-mortar base of a school or university is at a significant point in time. In our highly networked society, virtual worlds provide a bridge between the 2D web spaces such as Facebook and Twitter and the 3D physical spaces of the classroom. People can come together as avatars to experience the same activity at the same time regardless of any physical limitations such as geographical location or personal attributes. This provides teachers and students with opportunities to connect and collaborate in ways that were previously unimaginable.

Change and innovation

Change and innovation has been a consistent theme in education (Cuban, 1984; Hargreaves, 2005). Since the 1960s, several reforms have been implemented, reviewed and, in turn, abandoned in a continuous attempt to cater for the perceived needs of learners. Fullan (1993) suggested that the way in which the 'concept of educational change' is discussed and approached needs to be reassessed to reconcile the 'juxtaposition of a continuous change theme with a continuous conservative [education] system' (p. 3). It is commonly accepted that, for innovation and change to be facilitated in education, teachers need to be supported to think in creative ways about the nature of teaching and learning. With the exponential rise in the inclusion of technology in universities, schools and the everyday lives of individuals, the role that technology plays in education needs to be at the forefront of this support.

Adopting a new technology can occur at different times within any one institution. Some faculty and teachers will be innovators who take quickly to finding ways to integrate new technologies, while others wait to see the results and adopt later in the implementation cycle. Aldunate and Nussbaum (2013) found that the 'interplay between the type of user, based on their attitude towards new technology, and the type of technology, in terms of complexity of use' had a significant effect in determining the level of adoption that the teacher undertook (p. 524). They found that early adopters, who spend time integrating technology, are 'more likely to adopt new technology, regardless of its complexity', whereas those who are not early adopters and don't commit time to integrating technology 'are prone to abandoning the adoption at identified points in the process' (p. 519). These early adopters need to be supported through their period of experimentation in order that the innovation can continue and flourish.

Barriers

The integration of emerging technologies has consistently encountered similar barriers and, despite these being identified and documented, they continue to present hurdles for educators. In 1993, Cuban (1993) made comparisons between education and the uptake of technology that was occurring in other industries. He observed that there were two factors that had a significant impact on the capacity of teachers in schools to integrate technology, namely: (1) the cultural view of what 'proper schooling' is (beliefs about teaching, learning and knowledge shaped not just by scholars in the discipline but by various members of society); and (2) the structure of school (in particular, the age-based segregation of learning). These two factors highlight the influence that stakeholders have in shaping what happens in education as well as the institutional factors that can affect the teacher's capacity to implement innovations when they must 'fit the contours of these age-graded settings' (Cuban, 1993, p. 186). If we were to remove these structures in schools, we would be looking at a very different system that has a greater capacity to support innovative technology and pedagogies.

The restrictions that can occur through the nature of schools (and universities) are part of what Ertmer (1999) calls first-order barriers: those that are external to the person. In her early work, she generalized barriers to technology use into two main areas: first-order barriers and second-order barriers. The second-order barriers were internal and more able to be resolved or controlled by the individual. Ertmer found that, in ITE, attempts to overcome first-order barriers were given the most attention with a strong focus on providing access to equipment and programmes teaching specific technology skills. There was a belief that 'if teachers had access to enough equipment and training, classroom integration would follow' (p. 47). Over time, she (Ertmer & Ottenbreit-Leftwich, 2013) has found that simply providing the equipment and the skills was not enough to facilitate a change in practice. Ertmer and Ottenbreit-Leftwich (2013) suggest that the focus needs to be on the 'pedagogy that technology enables, rather than on the technology itself' (p. 175). One of the main reasons that a shift away from focusing on first-order barriers is more appropriate today is that many of these barriers (resources, training, support) have been alleviated with money and effort channelled into increasing resources, training and support in K-12 and university education.

The second-order barriers that Ertmer described have been noted in other studies (Baskin & Williams, 2006; Bitner & Bitner, 2002; Gill & Dalgarno, 2008; Gulbahar, 2008; Prestridge, 2012; Wang, 2002). They are the internal barriers or 'human factors' that include the individual's attitudes and beliefs, knowledge and skills. These second-order barriers have been found to be highly influential and affect the content and delivery of ITE programmes. Baskin and Williams (2006) claimed 'the human factor is perceived as the most critical in nurturing the technology culture and growing the critical mass of teachers able to sustain the use of technology effectively in their teaching' (p. 465). These human factors were identified by Bitner and Bitner (2002) as: a fear of change, a need for training in basic skills, their personal use, the teaching models provided, the technology to be based in learning activities, the school culture, intrinsic and extrinsic motivation and the level of support. In addition to these, Vrasidas and Glass (2005) emphasize 'the conservative nature of the traditional culture of schooling and classroom instruction' as well as the 'lack of time for teachers to learn how to use and integrate technology into their teaching' (p. 8). The impact that teachers' current beliefs and practices have on their capacity to integrate technology is so intrinsic that Vrasidas and Glass (2005, p. 8) suggest that teachers need to 'unlearn' these traditional practices before they can move to new ways of integrating technology. Changing traditional practice can be difficult for many teachers and Prestridge

(2012) found that they were often able to overcome the first-order barriers; however, the digital pedagogies required for effective implementation were not adopted.

There is an important interplay between ITE faculty, students and K–12 classroom teachers in their attitudes towards the role that technology plays in an educational setting. At each stage, the attitude of the individual has the capacity to influence those that they teach. The way that technology use is modelled in ITE teacher programmes influences the capacity of the ITE student to integrate and innovate when entering the profession. Wang (2002) identified the role that ITE faculty play in developing capacity for ITE students and indicated that helping the ITE students to have a 'clear vision of their roles as a teacher' (p. 150) who uses technology was a major factor in the future integration. Fundamentally we, in ITE, need to be innovating and integrating so that students will have a greater capacity to do so in the 'traditional' classroom and influence the practices of the profession.

What are virtual worlds?

Throughout the literature, in the mass media and in everyday language, the term virtual worlds is used to describe a variety of spaces that exist as 'virtual'. The virtual worlds referred to in this book are the 3D virtual worlds of the type that are synonymous with platforms such as Second Life and OpenSim. Gregory et al. (2013) define them as 'a computer-based, immersive, 3D multi-user environment that simulates real (or imaginary) life, experienced through a graphical representation of the user' (p. 314). I acknowledge that there are many games that would be considered virtual worlds as per this definition; however, the virtual worlds I am most interested in are the ones in which the user can create within the space and that are not defined by game-based structures. My reason for choosing open, user-created worlds is that faculty, teachers and students might utilize these spaces to develop their own knowledge and/or to design learning experiences rather than being given a space with pre-defined experiences.

There has been a great deal of interest in the use of virtual worlds in education but very little empirical research or documentation that can be replicated across contexts. Educational researchers have suggested that for virtual worlds to become more widespread in the sector, a systematic study into how and why virtual worlds are important needs to be undertaken. While Dede (2009) suggested 'further studies are needed on the capabilities of immersive media for learning, on the instructional design best suited to each type of immersive medium, and on the learning strengths and preferences these media develop in users' (p. 66), few studies have emerged since this time. Similarly, Dalgarno and Lee (2010) argued that there was a need for 'a concerted and systematic effort by researchers to ascertain whether or not, and if so, how, the capabilities and features of 3D VLEs can be exploited in pedagogically sound ways' (p. 23). Their call for links to sound pedagogy have also yielded little in the way of actual examples and outcomes, with Dalgarno, Gregory, Carlson, Lee and Tynan (2013) reporting that 'while much has been written in recent years about the possible benefits of virtual worlds for learning, evidence of the actual learning benefits is sparse' (p. 18).

The period between 2007 and 2010 was a time when a significant number of higher education institutions were utilizing Second Life as a learning space; it might be considered the 'heyday' of virtual worlds in higher education. In 2007, virtual worlds were cited in the New Media Consortium's Horizon Report as being within two to three years of adoption in higher education (NMC, 2007):

> Virtual worlds can be used to create very effective learning spaces. Since they are generalized rather than contextual, they are applicable to almost all disciplines. Settings can be created to pertain to any subject or area of study; locations and artefacts can be as realistic and detailed, or as generic and undefined as desired. 3D construction tools allow easy visualization of physical objects and materials, even those normally occurring at cosmic or nano scales.
>
> (NMC, 2007, p. 20)

Furthermore, claims were made by information technology research and advisory company Gartner that 'by the end of 2011, 80 per cent of active Internet users (and Fortune 500 enterprises) will have a "Second Life", but not necessarily in Second Life' (Gartner, 2007). At the end of 2011, there were approximately 1.7 billion registered virtual world accounts (KZero, 2012) and 2 billion active Internet users worldwide. In 2014, there were approximately 2.8 billion registered virtual world accounts and almost 3 billion Internet users (ITU, 2014). During 2016, the interest in virtual reality increased with the introduction of hardware that is suitable for home use, at an affordable price. Second Life maintains a large user base, with 50 million accounts created and regular users around 1 million a month (Voyager, 2017). However, as Gartner predicted, there are many people with 'Second Lives' on other platforms, such as in games (e.g. Minecraft, World of Warcraft) and OpenSim environments (e.g. Kitely, OpenSim).

While use across virtual world platforms remains fairly high and is increasing, there has been a decrease in interest and investment from the higher education sector. Lowendahl (2013) stated that the position of virtual worlds in education had 'diminished in higher education circles' (p. 68) because Second Life was not interesting enough for most faculty. Although he did believe that there had been some successes, especially with the use of other virtual worlds 'for the purpose of creating experiences that can take place only in virtual environments' (p. 68). The 2016 Gartner Hype Cycle for education puts virtual worlds in the Plateau of Productivity, suggesting that they are moving towards being utilized in a way that has shifted beyond that of a novelty.

Interestingly, in 2007, Kapp (2007) wrote a blog post in which he reflected on the similarities between the backlash occurring in education against virtual worlds and the backlash that occurred at the 'birth of e-learning'. He describes the hype that surrounded e-learning that led to academics claiming 'e-learning was expensive to build, complicated and boring. The return on investment wasn't worth it and several high profile online universities closed their doors ... it was the end of e-learning' (para. 3). He goes on to recall that a 'small group of dedicated people, university departments and companies' ignored the hype and continued with e-learning developments (para. 4). Kapp (2007) suggested that virtual worlds were in a similar position as they had been subjected to over-hyping and in the long term their true potential would be realized. I. Christensen, Maraunchak and Stefanelli (2013) also draw similarities to the barriers that occurred in the early years of web-based, distance-learning programmes. They believed that 'the focus remains on educational methodology and processes as ways to improve learning outcomes, and few resources are spent on investigating the technical aspects of e-learning platforms, standards, and the myriad of technical offers' (Chapter 11, para. 4). This reminds us that while new technologies continue to arise with promise of great progress in education, it is the individual, the faculty, teacher and student who need to see the ways to utilize the technology for the benefit and the sustainability of the technology in a teaching and learning environment.

Starting out with virtual worlds

My first use of a virtual world for teaching occurred in 2010 while writing a new unit of study as part of a redesign towards a blended delivery mode (one that included on-campus and online delivery). An important aspect of the new unit was to unite three geographically separate student cohorts. Previously the cohorts had been provided with separate tutors and, as the student cohorts had diminished in size, this mode of delivery was not cost effective. In that same year, the university developed a virtual campus in

Second Life for all faculty and students to explore the possibilities of the virtual world in education. The use of the virtual world in Second Life provided a way to bring all the students together, in one space, where they would be able to discuss discipline-specific concepts and explore new technology. As I began to use Second Life, it became clear that there were several factors influencing the students' ability and willingness to engage in the use of virtual worlds as part of their studies. The mixed reaction from the students, faculty and university management was not what I expected and opened up a series of new questions for me to explore.

Second Life was chosen, by the university, as it offered a stable and mature platform with a market place from which ready-made objects could be purchased as well as an extensive network of pre-existing communities and simulation resources suitable for teaching and learning. It was relatively easy to sign up to and required little to no support from the university's information technology for faculty and students to participate. An innovation grant had been awarded to develop a virtual campus for use by the university faculty and students and the virtual campus, Interaction Island, was designed and built.

Interaction Island was deliberately built with features that looked similar to the physical university campus. This was to provide a space that faculty and students would feel some familiarity with, to alleviate any initial uneasiness presented by the significant strangeness of the virtual world. Access was restricted to university faculty and students who registered with the administrator to encourage them to visit and explore a virtual world in a safe setting. The use of Second Life had raised issues for the faculty and students due to mainstream publicity about the types of activities that people undertook in that space, as being anti-social and not considered educational. Thus, creating a space that behaved more like the university-controlled learning management system (LMS) was one way to minimize these concerns.

In the first year of operation, there was a great deal of interest in Interaction Island and various faculties in the university were curious about how they could use the space for their programmes. As such, two more islands were established: Commerce Town, which had a series of businesses situated around one main street designed primarily for Business, Tourism and Hospitality; and DBA Island for the Doctor of Business Administration programme. When I began my research in ITE I used Interaction Island, and then a space on the Business Island. I successfully received a grant to develop an island dedicated to ITE and I planned a fourth island. During this process, the DBA programme realized that they were no longer going to use their island and we repurposed the island for ITE. This illustrates one of the capacities of virtual worlds in which complete spaces can be demolished and rebuilt at very little cost compared to a rebuild in the physical 'bricks and mortar' world.

The first significant use of Interaction Island was with the cohort of ITE students studying to be visual arts teachers in secondary schools. At that time, the Bachelor of Education (Secondary) degree programme was part of a university-wide trial to offer students a wider variety of study options. The inclusion of a virtual world, to unite three disparate cohorts, offered an opportunity to explore an innovative technological solution. Following on from this was the inclusion of virtual worlds in: Science and Technology Education; Learning Technologies; Curriculum, Assessment and New Media; Human Society and its Environments; Curriculum and Pedagogy; Early Childhood Foundations; and Instructional Design and Educational Technology. Each of these represents discrete units in the ITE programme. A unit is similar to what might be termed a subject or a course in an international university. A unit typically consists of up to 150 hours of study per term or semester. In the context of this research, the units have ten designated teaching weeks to allow for three practicum weeks when students are in schools. Typically each unit will have ten one-hour lectures and ten two-hour tutorials. Students are generally expected to spend up to ten hours of study for one unit each week (including the lecture and tutorial/workshop). Virtual world activities in these units included – virtual field trips, tutorial discussions, building a sustainable design project, role-play and developing virtual world teaching and learning resources. This book provides case studies from these units with descriptions and discussion based on research and reflections from students and faculty.

Research

The research discussed in this book was undertaken in the ITE programme at an Australian public, regional university. The university provides ITE from three campuses in on-campus (face-to-face), online and blended delivery modes. With close to 15,000 students, the university is one of the smallest in Australia. The student cohort is approximately 30 per cent online, 20 per cent school leavers, 23 per cent have low socio-economic status and 3.4 per cent are Indigenous.

The choice of the research site was opportunistic, as I have worked at the university as a sessional lecturer, tutor, marker and unit designer since 2009. The timing of this research was influenced by the opportunity for me to be the first person to utilize virtual worlds in my teaching. This provided me with the ideal environment in which to investigate how a new technology could be introduced, developed and supported. Furthermore, being situated in an ITE programme provided a chance to analyse the types of pedagogies that faculty and students expected to utilize when integrating innovative technologies.

My methodology is based in an action research meta-methodology in which I situate myself as a participant researcher. Davis and Sumara (2006) suggest that educational research should be exploring the 'current spaces of possibility' as part of the goal of being 'oriented toward the as-yet unimagined' (p. 135). I was immediately drawn to their vision of educational research as it synthesized my own view about what I should be doing as a teacher and a researcher. Their statement struck a chord with me when they said 'Education – and, by implication, educational research – conceived in terms of expanding the space of the possible rather than perpetuating entrenched habits of interpretation, then, must be principally concerned with ensuring the conditions for the emergence of the as-yet unimagined' (p. 135). Working with innovative technologies in spaces that faculty and students are unfamiliar with has the potential to break the mould of expected pedagogical approaches.

Conclusion

This book provides insight into some of the ways that virtual worlds can be integrated into higher education. Research was conducted in the ITE programme at an Australian university where more than 1,000 students and six faculty were introduced to virtual worlds for their teaching, learning and future practice. From this research, feedback was analysed to reveal the complexities of integrating innovative technology. By reading this book, you will find practical examples of how virtual worlds were introduced and supported as well as reflections from faculty and students about their response to virtual worlds.

References

Aldunate, R., & Nussbaum, M. (2013). Teacher adoption of technology. *Computers in Human Behavior, 29*(3), 519–524.

Apple, M. W. (2014). *Official knowledge: Democratic education in a conservative age* (3rd ed.). New York: Routledge.

Baskin, C., & Williams, M. (2006). ICT integration in schools: Where are we now and what comes next? *Australasian Journal of Educational Technology, 22*(4), 455–473.

Bitner, N., & Bitner, J. (2002). Integrating technology into the classroom: Eight keys to success. *Journal of Technology and Teacher Education, 10*(1), 95–100.

Christensen, C. M., Horn, M. B., & Johnson, C. W. (2011). *Disrupting class: How disruptive innovation will change the way the world learns.* New York: McGraw Hill.

Christensen, I., Maraunchak, A., & Stefanelli, C. (2013). Added value of teaching in a virtual world. In R. Teigland & D. Power (Eds.), *The immersive internet: Reflections on the entangling of the virtual with society, politics and the economy* (pp. 125–137). Hampshire, UK: Palgrave Macmillan.

Cuban, L. (1984). *How teachers taught: Constancy and change in American classrooms, 1890–1980.* New York: Longman.

Cuban, L. (1993). Computers meet classroom: Classroom wins. *The Teachers College Record, 95*(2), 185–210.

Dalgarno, B., & Lee, M. J. W. (2010). What are the learning affordances of 3-D virtual environments? *British Journal of Educational Technology, 41*(1), 10–32.

Dalgarno, B., Gregory, S., Carlson, L., Lee, M. J. W., & Tynan, B. (2013). *A systematic review and environmental analysis of the use of 3D immersive virtual worlds in Australian and New Zealand higher education institutions. Final report 2013.* www.researchgate.net/publication/279205705.

Davis, B., & Sumara, D. (2006). *Complexity and education: Inquiries into learning, teaching, and research.* New Jersey: Psychology Press.

Dede, C. (2009). Immersive interfaces for engagement and learning. *Science, 323*(5910), 66–69.

Ertmer, P. A. (1999). Addressing first- and second-order barriers to change: Strategies for technology integration. *Educational Technology Research and Development, 47*(4), 47–61.

Ertmer, P. A., & Ottenbreit-Leftwich, A. (2013). Removing obstacles to the pedagogical changes required by Jonassen's vision of authentic technology-enabled learning. *Computers & Education, 64*, 175–182.

Fullan, M. (1993). Why teachers must become change agents. *Educational Leadership, 50*, 12–17.

Gartner. (2007). Gartner says 80 percent of active internet users will have a 'Second Life' in the virtual world by the end of 2011. www.gartner.com/it/page.jsp?id=503861.

Gill, L., & Dalgarno, B. (2008). Influences on pre-service teachers' preparedness to use ICTs in the classroom. In R. Atkinson & C. McBeath (Eds.), *Hello! Where are you in the landscape of educational technology? Proceedings of ascilite 2008* (pp. 330–339). Melbourne, Australia: Deakin University.

Goodman, J. (2012). *Reforming schools: Working within a progressive tradition during conservative times.* New York: SUNY Press.

Gregory, S., Gregory, B., Reiners, T., Hillier, M., Lee, M. J. W., Jacka, L., ... Larson, I. (2013). Virtual worlds in Australian and New Zealand higher education: Remembering the past, understanding the present and imagining the future. In H. Carter, M. Gosper & J. Hedberg (Eds.), *Electric dreams. Proceedings of ascilite 2013* (pp. 312–324). Sydney: Macquarie University.

Gulbahar, Y. (2008). ICT usage in higher education: A case study on preservice teachers and instructors. *The Turkish Online Journal of Educational Technology, 7*(1), 32–37.

Hargreaves, A. (2005). The emotions of teaching and educational change. In A. Hargreaves (Ed.), *Extending educational change* (pp. 278–295). Dordrecht: Springer.

Hargreaves, A., & Shirley, D. (2012). *The global fourth way: The quest for educational excellence*. Thousand Oaks, CA: SAGE.

ITU. (2014). *The world in 2014: ICT facts and figures*. www.itu.int/en/ITU-D/Statistics/Documents/facts/ICTFactsFigures2014-e.pdf.

Kapp, K. (2007). The metaverse hype, decline and realism cycle: We've seen it before. [blog] http://karlkapp.com/metaverse-hype-decline-and-realism/.

KZero. (2012). Virtual world registered accounts reach 1.7bn in Q4 2011. [blog] www.kzero.co.uk/blog/virtual-world-registered-accounts-reach-1-7bn-q4-2011/.

Lowendahl, J. M. (2013). *Hype cycle for education*. www.gartner.com/doc/2559615/hype-cycle-education-.

NMC. (2007). *The horizon report 2007 edition*. www.nmc.org/publication/nmc-horizon-report-2007-higher-ed-edition/.

Prestridge, S. (2012). The beliefs behind the teacher that influences their ICT practices. *Computers & Education, 58*(1), 449–458.

Voyager, D. (2017). Second Life grid statistics. https://danielvoyager.wordpress.com/2017/07/05/second-life-grid-statistics-summer-update-2017/.

Vrasidas, C., & Glass, G. V. (2005). *Preparing teachers to teach with technology*. Charlotte, NC: IAP.

Wang, Y. M. (2002). When technology meets beliefs: Preservice teachers' perception of the teacher's role in the classroom with computers. *Journal of Research on Technology in Education, 35*(1), 150–161.

1 Virtual worlds

1.1 Introduction

The definition of virtual worlds has been consistently evolving in response to the changes that have occurred in virtual world applications, computer hardware and networking capabilities. Bell (2008) described virtual worlds as 'a synchronous, persistent network of people, represented as avatars, facilitated by networked computers' (p. 2) while Warburton (2009) identified virtual worlds as having six distinct features:

1　Persistence of the in-world environment
2　A shared space allowing multiple users to participate simultaneously
3　Virtual embodiment in the form of an avatar (a personalizable 3D representation of the self)
4　Interactions that occur between users and objects in a 3D environment
5　An immediacy of action such that interactions occur in real time
6　Similarities to the real world, such as topography, movement and physics that provide the illusion of being there

(p. 245)

Both definitions relate to the virtual worlds that were most commonly being used in 2008/2009, such as Second Life. Gregory et al. (2013) defined virtual worlds as 'a computer-based, immersive, 3D multi-user environment that simulates real (or imaginary) life, experienced through a graphical representation of the user' (p. 314). This definition was agreed upon after some discussion between members of the Australia and New Zealand Virtual Worlds Working Group (VWWG). This group was established in 2009 and represents over 200 faculty that are either using or are interested in using virtual worlds in higher education. During these discussions, it became clear that faculty were using a range of virtual worlds that displayed different characteristics; however, there were common factors that helped to identify the specific genre of virtual world that these faculty were using; primarily Second Life and OpenSim worlds in which the user could create content.

Some of the issues that arose from the discussion included whether the virtual world is the opposite of the real world or whether the virtual world can be considered real. Of concern was whether virtual learning environments (VLEs), such as the LMS that most universities use (e.g. Blackboard or Moodle), are virtual worlds or whether online applications such as Facebook, Google Earth or Google Sketch Up are also virtual worlds. The most significant difference between these applications and the types of virtual worlds that most members of the VWWG were using is the 'experience through a graphical representation of the user' (i.e. an avatar). The inclusion of the avatar is significant as it promotes the synchronous experience that is similar to being with a group of people (students and faculty) in an 'on-campus' or 'real' environment.

1.2 Evolution

Computer-mediated environments that facilitate immersion of the user in a 3D space have been written about since the 1950s (Bradbury, 1951; Knight, 1952) and were rudimentarily pioneered in the 1960s with the design and development of Heilig's *Sensorama* and Sutherland and Sproull's *The Sword of Damocles* head-mounted display (Sutherland, 1965, 1968). In broad terms, these experiences have been labelled virtual reality (VR). Today the terms VR and virtual worlds are often interchangeable; however, VR is more commonly used to refer to experiences in which the user is physically immersed in a computer-simulated environment and virtual world is more likely to include environments in which the user is embodied as an avatar and interacts within the space through a mouse (or other handheld device such as a 'joy stick'), keyboard and screen (computer or TV monitor).

Development of VR continues with discoveries and developments informing much of the current popular entertainment experiences, such as the Kinect, Wii, Xbox, Google Cardboard and Oculus Rift. The entertainment industry has helped to spearhead the development of VR and virtual worlds; however, the potential for the application to education has been consistently noted. In 1962, Heilig, as part of his patent for Sensorama, mentioned that he believed that his device could meet the 'increasing demands today for ways and means to teach and train individuals without actually subjecting the individuals to the hazards of particular simulations' (cited in Heilig, 1992, p. 292).

The range of VR experiences and environments can be classified in a variety of ways. Tice and Jacobson (1992, p. 281) suggested three types of implementation – immersive, desktop and third-person.

> *Immersive* VR requires the user to wear equipment that facilitates the immersive experience by blocking out the real world and projecting image and audio through head mounted displays, gloves, position tracking devices and 3D sound systems.

> *Desktop* VR is experienced through a 'window' as the user looks onto the VR space and steers themselves through that space.

> *Third-person* VR is one in which the user sees themselves within the space and steers their persona while viewing from the aspect of a third person.

The three categories proposed by Tice and Jacobson in 1992 can still be applied to today's VR, yet the way the user interacts with VR has changed to become smaller, faster and more immersive, even within a desktop or third-person environment. With the rapid development of consumer-level technology that delivers high-speed processing, high-definition audio-visuals and high-speed Internet connectivity, access to VR is now a reality for most users at home, work, school or university. This level of access has significant implications for the way that we use VR and the pressing need to integrate VR in education.

Many of the virtual worlds marketed at children, such as Club Penguin and Moshi Monsters, promote themselves as having educational content to attract parental consent. They include structured educational games within the open-ended worlds and entice the children to play the games with rewards of points that can be used to buy products within the virtual world. The ability to chat can be prevented if the parent chooses that level of restriction. The child can be given options of dialogue to choose, such as 'hello' or 'how are you?', to remove the potential for any chat that might be of an inappropriate nature, such as adults posing as children and grooming children. These concerns about virtual worlds from the adult's perspective are significant when virtual worlds are being utilized in a classroom setting. The publicity surrounding virtual worlds as spaces that can be inhabited by adults using avatars to portray a certain persona and interacting in anti-social behaviour presents a barrier that is not encountered when other new technology is first introduced in a classroom setting.

Despite the negative publicity, higher education institutions have primarily used the virtual world Second Life. The concerns that parents have in relation to their children using these spaces is not applicable to those that are part of the adult learning environment. However, adult students have still expressed some concerns about the safety of Second Life. Helmer (2007) proposed several reasons why Second Life was worth investigating for teaching and learning in higher education, including that it has a pre-existing engine (hosted technical infrastructure), a global reach, a wide range of interest groups/communities and augmented capability (users can teleport, fly, see around corners), it is media rich and links externally to the 2D web, and it has easy-to-use building tools, a rapidly evolving platform and user-created content. One of the benefits of Second Life for education is the user-created content that forms an extensive network of ready-made immersive environments and objects that can be visited, copied, modified and transferred for specific teaching and learning scenarios. Second Life has no pre-defined goals or levels to achieve and participants can create any in-world environment they imagine with the available in-world tools.

Until 2011 Second Life was the 'most popular virtual world used by faculty' (Farley, 2011, p. 382). However, with the removal of the education tiered pricing, in January 2011, and a reduction in the creative and technical support for faculty, many started to look at other platforms. OpenSimulator (OpenSim) is one platform that has proven popular due, in part, to the ability to host the virtual world locally or to purchase parcels of land (server space) relatively inexpensively on pre-formatted servers (e.g. JokaydiaGRID or Kitely). In response to the loss of educators to other virtual world platforms, Linden Labs reinstated the education discount in 2013; however, the shift to more education-friendly spaces appears to have already occurred, with the number of regions in OpenSim tripling between 2010 and 2013 (Kariuki, 2017).

OpenSim is an 'open source multi-platform, multi-user 3D application server. It can be used to create a virtual environment (or world) which can be accessed through a variety of clients, on multiple protocols' (OpenSimulator, 2017, para. 1). OpenSim virtual worlds have similar characteristics to other content creation virtual worlds such as Second Life, making them an ideal platform to transfer to from Second Life. However, they do require a higher level of technical knowledge if the user is to set up a server and host an OpenSim environment.

Second Life has never been an option in K-6 schools due to age restrictions imposed by Second Life (minimum age of thirteen) and networking restrictions imposed by Departments of Education. Prior to 2011, Second Life hosted a teen grid on which faculty and children aged 13–18 could design and use learning activities. However, the Second Life teen grid was removed in January 2011. As a result of these restrictions, some K-12 schools set up locally hosted OpenSim environments. This has only been possible in schools that have the technical and financial support to do so.

To overcome the barriers of technical expertise and access to networked servers, Sim-on-a-Stick (SoaS) was developed by a team of interested computer programmers. SoaS is based on the OpenSim architecture with the added capacity to be accessed from a USB flash drive with no require-ment for an Internet connection. The virtual world spaces are hosted on a USB flash drive (or similar non-networked device) and uses MySQL as the server. When the user first enters SoaS, they are provided with one or more flat regions on which they can build. Ready-made environments and objects can be freely acquired from several OpenSim creators and loaded into individual spaces. If a teacher or student has built an environment, or objects, that they wish to share they can export their builds to be imported into other users' sims. While some of these functions require more exper-tise than others, there is a strong community of OpenSim users who provide information. All of these features have made SoaS a viable option for K-12 and university environments in which the networked social virtual worlds can present issues for students and teachers.

1.3 Affordances

As educational researchers have attempted to identify the ways in which technology can offer a different teaching and learning experience, the concept of affordance has provided the language to describe unique features. Once an affordance of a technology is identified, the educator is better able to provide concrete reasons why they would choose to use the technology in lieu of a previously accepted educational tool, resource or technique. They may also find that the affordance that the technology was first intended for is not as they end up using it as they imagine ways to extend both their ped-agogical approach and the limitations of the technology.

The term 'affordance' was coined by Gibson (1979) and has been appro-priated in various contexts, with subtly different meanings. Gibson first sug-gested that an affordance was inherent within an object. The affordance was that which the object was designed to do (e.g. a ball was designed to be thrown). On the other hand, Norman (1988) used the term affordance to include that which the user may perceive the object could be used for. His idea was one of 'perceived affordance' and focused on the usability of an object (e.g. a ball may be designed to be thrown but a person may choose to sit on the ball and use it as a seat). Norman's work was influential with those involved in human computer interface (HCI) design as he stressed that, while objects are designed for a purpose, the user may interact with objects in unintended ways. As such the designer of a HCI must at first approach the object as having the affordance most likely to be considered by the user, but may end up with the user finding a different purpose.

This use of 'affordance' was applied by Bower (2008) in his discussion of the usefulness of considering affordances of educational technology in the design process; he suggested, 'determining technological affordances before considering tasks can lead to unnecessary analysis' (p. 9). He recommends that the educational designer should consider the affordance requirements of the task with knowledge of the affordances of the technology to avoid the development of impractical implementation. In his model, the educational outcomes are placed before the educational tool. This is a pertinent point to make, as there are often times when technology is seen as the solution without consideration for the pedagogy. However, an understanding of the technological affordances of a particular resource may also lead to unexpected uses and the development of innovative tasks.

Pedagogical affordances of 3D VLEs is something that Dalgarno and Lee (2010) looked for when describing the 3D VLEs such as 3D simulations, games and other 3D virtual environments. They claimed that the 'tasks, activities and underpinning pedagogical strategies' (p. 17) that can be facilitated using a 3D VLE has the most impact on learning. As such they sought to identify the learning affordances that 3D VLEs offer as unique from other types of VLEs (such as 2D VLEs that include learning management systems used in universities). From their review of the literature, they concluded that there were five learning affordances:

1   Learning tasks that lead to the development of enhanced spatial knowledge representation of the explored domain
2   Experiential learning tasks that would be impractical or impossible to undertake in the real world
3   Learning tasks that lead to increased intrinsic motivation and engagement
4   Learning tasks that lead to improved transfer of knowledge and skills to real situations through contextualization of learning
5   Tasks that lead to richer and/or more effective collaborative learning than is possible with 2D alternatives

(p. 17)

Each of these learning affordances is supported by the 3D VLE's ability to provide effective representational fidelity and the ability for the learner to interact with artefacts and other users within the shared space. The learner is experiencing the task or activity through the embodiment of an avatar and their suspension of disbelief about the physical reality of the space. This interaction as an avatar generates a sense of presence. On the other hand, 2D VLEs create a 'disembodied' way of learning and knowing in which the teacher and students are not viscerally in the same space (Dall'Alba & Barnacle, 2005).

Developing 'presence' is an important element in teaching and learning, whether virtually, on-campus or blended, as has been discussed by Garrison and Anderson (2003) as part of their Community of Inquiry framework. Garrison and Anderson (2003) suggested that it is important for teachers and students to share a sense of presence or co-presence within the educational space to enhance the learning experience. Warburton (2009) proposed that the virtual world has the capacity to create a 'profoundly immersive experience', one in which the teacher and student (as avatars) can reside simultaneously, thus providing 'a compelling educational experience, particularly in relation to simulation and role-playing activities' (p. 419).

Virtual presence has evolved from text-based chat rooms, in which participants interacted in real time by typing into their computers, through to web conferencing and VLEs that include text, video, still images and graphics. However, virtual worlds offer a new level of virtual presence, as Wenger, White and Smith (2009) describe in their reflection on the type of experience that an individual might have in Second Life:

> Seeing others' avatars, even if we do not interact with them, lets us know we are not alone. No one knows where this trend will lead, but it is clear that it has the potential to transform the way we interact, and more generally, the way we experience togetherness.
>
> (p. 175)

Facilitating the ability of faculty and students to have a similar sense of presence as if they were in a traditional face-to-face classroom yet in a VLE is only one of the affordances of virtual worlds. Warburton was one of the first researchers to provide a list of affordances for virtual worlds in education and his 2009 article is widely accepted as a seminal text. He suggested that virtual worlds have the potential to provide:

- extended or rich interactions
- visualization and contextualization
- authentic content and culture
- identity play
- immersion
- simulation
- community presence
- content production.

(p. 421)

There are unique opportunities that the use of virtual worlds in higher education can provide, as Savin-Baden (2011) proposed: (a) activities can be undertaken that, in real life, would be expensive, dangerous or impossible; (b) the use of the avatar can provide opportunities to play with roles and identities that encourage playfulness and a testing of boundaries; and (c) as a result there is more likely to be experimentation as most actions in the virtual world have little or no real-life consequences.

The visual aspect of virtual worlds helps to redefine 'the landscape of online interaction away from text and toward a more complex visual medium that provides a sense of place, space, and physiological embodiment' (Thomas & Seely-Brown, 2009, p. 2). An affordance that Thomas and Seely-Brown credited to the virtual world was the capacity for the user to 'shape and to a large extent create the world they inhabit' (p. 1). This ability for the user to create in the virtual world has significant consequences for changing the current model of teaching and learning in higher education.

What is important, as shown in the literature, is for technology to be effectively utilized in the educational context; the role technology plays in supporting learning must not be overshadowed by the technology itself. Clark (1994) suggested, in the early 1990s, when the use of multimedia resources was being seen as a solution to engage students in learning, that if the same learning outcome could be derived from more than one type of media then it was not the media that was the influencing factor but more so the delivery of the learning activity. Clark was highly critical of claims being made by faculty that different forms of media could have a causal effect on student's learning. This same observation could be applied to contemporary technological innovations as we see faculty use technology that is not always producing better learning outcomes. The question, then, is whether it is the technology or the pedagogy that is producing these outcomes.

In relation to virtual worlds, there is value in highlighting the affordances that are unique to the technology of virtual worlds (some that are very different to previous media and technology) and connecting them to the teaching and learning affordances of virtual worlds. Clearly providing these affordances to the ITE faculty and students gives them reasons to overcome any initial barriers to move towards a deeper level of understanding about how and why virtual worlds can be utilized. Being able to clearly articulate the ways that virtual worlds will enhance the learning experience is an important step towards integration and sustainable use of virtual worlds.

1.4 Barriers

With the implementation of virtual worlds across education sectors, several reports and case studies have highlighted the barriers, problems or limitations that are impacting on the capacity for virtual worlds to be more fully adopted. An early report undertaken by NMC (2007) surveyed 209 higher education faculty and identified some of the negative experiences they encountered as: technical issues, grieving, communication issues, a feeling of isolation or being lost and feeling embarrassed. Also in 2007 the US-based EDUCAUSE Center for Applied Research (ECAR) released a research bulletin (Kelton, 2007) that provided an overview of the institutions which were using Second Life. The main concern raised in this report was that Second Life can appear to not be a serious place for learning because 'those involved in Second Life appear to be having fun' (p. 8). In the following year, Kelton (2008) produced a report that identified barriers that were situated within the perceptual, technical, operational and pedagogical.

In the UK, the Joint Information Systems Committee (JISC) commissioned a scoping study (de Freitas, 2008) that included an overview of the challenges being experienced by faculty who were using virtual worlds. De Freitas (2008) reported that the main challenges were 'accessibility and the need for broadband capability, the requirement for open standards and more support for tutors and practitioners aiming to use virtual worlds such as guidelines, case studies and implementation models' (p. 30). She noted that the necessary shift to exploratory learning as the main form of teaching in a virtual world presented its own challenge for 'teaching practitioners well versed in traditional approaches to learning where information transferal from tutor to learner is more characteristic' (p. 30). Between 2007 and 2012 Virtual World Watch produced ten snapshot surveys, each providing an overview of the institutional use and attitude towards virtual worlds in the UK (Kirriemuir, 2017). While attitudes appear to have changed to some extent, some of the challenges remained over the five-year period, including the level of 'institutional support, such as information technology provision and virtual world access, faculty time, virtual world technology acceptability, and funding for faculty and infrastructure' (Kirriemuir, 2012, Summary, para. 6). Other factors included the steep learning curve involved for faculty and students, and the perception that virtual worlds were a game environment not suitable for serious learning activities.

Warburton (2009) cited barriers to the adoption of virtual worlds in education, with particular reference to Second Life, as:

- Technical: bandwidth, hardware and firewalls, down time and lag, navigation, creating objects, manipulating one's avatar and developing a visual 3D grammar.
- Identity: the fluidity and playfulness inherent in identity construction can be disconcerting and confusing. Building social relations can be problematic.
- Culture: Second Life can be an isolating experience. Communities are not always easy to find and can be demanding to participate in. Second Life is a place of no limits, no boundaries and no restrictions on behaviour.
- Collaboration: cooperation and co-construction need to be scaffolded, and building trust and authenticity are critical factors for successful group activities.
- Time: even simple things can take a long time.
- Economic: a basic account is free but anything beyond simply being present in-world costs money: buying land to create teaching spaces; uploading images and textures; purchasing useful in-world tools; employing building and scripting expertise.
- Standards: the lack of open standards and interoperability between virtual world platforms potentially locks any investment, both time and economic, inside a single non-transferable setting.
- Scaffolding persistence and social discovery: the in-world profiles associated with each avatar provide a limited mechanism for the social discovery of others, resulting in the avatar being trapped at the centre of its own community.

(pp. 422–423)

Unfortunately, many of these barriers still exist today and have contributed to the slower than anticipated uptake of virtual worlds. Dudeney and Ramsay (2009) distilled these factors into four areas – institutional, pedagogical, technical and end-user. They suggested that, while Second Life provided an entry-level environment for higher education users, the perception of Second Life by some sections within an institution often made it difficult to get funding or other support. They found that faculty wishing to use Second Life often chose not to name Second Life as the virtual world to gain institutional support and funding. In relation to pedagogy, they found that faculty were concerned about how to manage student behaviour within the space; for example, how will the students ask questions if they can't raise their hands or how will they stop the students flying around the room? The perception that Second Life was a game environment was also a concern and a potential barrier for those wishing to have the virtual world recognized as a learning space. These barriers signify the perception that the faculty had in relation to replicating the type of teaching they were engaged in. The need for a shift in their pedagogical approach was clearly the most significant factor that would influence their capacity to utilize virtual worlds in their disciplines. Since Dudeney and Ramsay's study, the use of games in education and games-based learning has gained some credibility as a valid form of teaching and learning. However, a more recent survey undertaken by Duncan, Miller and Jiang (2012) reveals that there are still consistent barriers to the use of virtual worlds. They surveyed 100 published academic papers, reports and web-sites to distil the research and practices associated with virtual worlds. In relation to barriers they found:

- Second Life requires computers with high specifications, especially graphic cards and high RAM (random access memory, main memory). Internet broadband speed is also crucial to the use of virtual worlds.
- Students sometimes found it hard to concentrate on the learning activity.
- It can be hard for faculty to monitor the educational process due to the lack of body language for feedback.
- In-world activities, such as building objectives using prims, might have no value or relationship to students' real-life world.
- The use of virtual simulation for teaching purposes might be challenged by the use of simulation in the real world.
- Additional context information may be required, which may be distracting.
- Some virtual world participants find that their first visit is too over-whelming and unguided to provide a meaningful experience.
- New students are unaware of social norms within a virtual world and require some understanding of language usage and gesturing.
- Simply using a virtual world is not sufficient to improve cognitive outcomes.

(pp. 960–961)

Dalgarno, Gregory, Carlson, Lee and Tynan's (2013) scoping study in Australia and New Zealand asked users to 'list up to five general limitations/disadvantages of virtual worlds for university learning and teaching' (p. 109). From the responses, seven overarching categories were identified: technology; support, funding and time; usability and familiarity; equity and ethical issues; inherent limitations of virtual worlds; acceptance of virtual worlds; and management and planning. Newman et al. (2013) also investigated why faculty were not using virtual worlds in education. The issues they found were primarily related to the institution, including a lack of funding, technical support, teaching support or adequate level of technology. Blackmon (2014) described four specific categories for barriers: equipment challenges; in-world virtual world challenges; university readiness; and student readiness. What she found was that, despite the challenges, the university faculty in her study persisted with their use of virtual worlds because they believed 'the potential the technology has to provide an added dimension of interaction or a dynamic versus static connection … is greater than the toying, tinkering, and tweaking those types of technologies often require' (p. 16).

The literature cited here in identifying barriers is all derived from investigations of the use of virtual worlds in higher education. There was no distinction between disciplines and as such the potential to specifically identify barriers unique to ITE is open to investigation. Furthermore, the barriers to adoption that arise in K-12 educational settings have the potential to impact on ITE teachers' perceptions and experiences.

1.5 Potential

Studies have suggested that ITE programmes are often not successful in preparing ITE students to be effective in their integration of technology. For example, Kay (2006) felt that the numerous strategies utilized to implement technology in ITE education were 'complex, diverse, often conflicting, and rarely evaluated well' (p. 384). As a result, she suggested, 'to date, there is no consolidated picture on how to effectively introduce technology to ITE students' (p. 387) and that there was potential to provide an evaluation of strategies to help guide the development of ITE programmes' integration of technology. This suggestion is supported by Lawless and Pellegrino (2007), who found that the integration that does occur '… is often not guided by any substantial knowledge base derived from research about what works and why with regard to technology, teaching, and learning' (p. 576).

Underpinning these observations is that fundamentally the ITE student lacks the pedagogical approach to using the technology more so than any lack of skill. Hedberg (2011) believes that, despite the investment in hardware and software and in implementing strategies to improve the pedagogical approach of ITE students, 'there is so far little evidence of any radical shifts in learning and teaching arising from classroom use of technology' (p. 3). Henderson, Bellis, Cerovac and Lancaster (2013) proposed that 'it is not unreasonable to make the claim that ITE as a whole risks failing in their mission to adequately prepare prospective teacher graduates' (p. 69) in the implementation to utilize technology as an effective part of the pedagogy.

In Australia, the Teaching the Teachers for the Future (TTF) project (2011) looked for ways to address some of the issues in relation to the readiness of ITE students to utilize technology in the classroom. They identified that teachers required content knowledge, pedagogical knowledge and technological knowledge, and the skills to interweave these at any time. As a result of the TFF project, Koehler and Mishra's (2009) technological pedagogical content knowledge (TPCK) framework was adopted and has been applied in many of Australia's ITE programmes. Virtual worlds offer the possibility to unpack the technological pedagogical content knowledge of students who are introduced to them. The immersion in a space that requires a new pedagogical approach to be effective, one that is often more student-centred, provides the push for ITE faculty and students to rethink the pedagogical processes.

In terms of research, potential virtual worlds are in their infancy and, until the release of Dalgarno et al. (2013), there were no extensive studies that reported on the experience of faculty and students across Australia and New Zealand. Haycock and Kemp (2008) suggested that research was 'needed to fine-tune both the academic processes and administrative infrastructure necessary to develop and support' virtual worlds. They found that faculty and students were 'woefully unprepared and unsupported to manoeuvre in immersive space' such as virtual worlds. Having the skills and the support removes initial barriers and initiates greater attention to the learning affordances by which 'sound instructional design and pedagogy will prevail over the mere novelty of the technology' (Dalgarno & Lee, 2010, p. 27).

There is optimism amongst many virtual world educators, as Christensen, Maraunchak and Stefanelli (2013) state: 'the development of education in virtual worlds in the next five to ten years has the potential to radically change not only how we learn but also the face of education' (Chapter 11, para. 2). This will only happen if, as Consalvo and Ess (2011) suggest, we 'critically investigate them, asking thoughtful questions and using careful methods, to best arrive at an understanding of what virtual worlds are and can be' (p. 344).

1.6 Conclusion

ITE has an important role to play in the development of new ways of implementing pedagogy that are relevant to today's students. The literature reveals that ITE faculty are deeply concerned with providing opportunities for their students to overcome barriers to the integration of technology in their future classrooms. However, there is also scepticism in relation to new technologies due to the lack of in-depth, longitudinal research that links the ITE faculty, ITE student and the K-12 teacher's experiences. Laurillard, Oliver, Wasson and Hoppe (2009) suggest that education systems are 'still in the relatively early stages of mainstream implementation of digital technologies for enhancing learning' (p. 304). They believe that the full potential of technology will only be realized through the 'building and sharing' of knowledge about the 'implementation of digital technologies for enhancing learning' (p. 304). This connection between the technology and learning needs to be explored from a variety of perspectives to fully understand the breadth of experiences and diversity of learning. The power of virtual worlds is yet to be realized and research to continue to support the implementation needs to occur so that virtual worlds do not become another new technology that is replaced by the next new technology without being fully explored in a systematic manner.

1.7 References

Bell, M. W. (2008). Toward a definition of 'virtual worlds'. *Journal of Virtual Worlds Research, 1*(1), 1–5.

Blackmon, S. (2014). Professors and Second Life: Technology problems and reasons for persistence. *International Higher Education Teaching and Learning Association, 4.*

Bower, M. (2008). Affordance analysis: Matching learning tasks with learning technologies. *Educational Media International, 45*(1), 3–15.

Bradbury, R. (1951). The veldt. In *The illustrated man* (pp. 7–25). New York: Doubleday and Company.

Christensen, I., Maraunchak, A., & Stefanelli, C. (2013). Added value of teaching in a virtual world. In R. Teigland & D. Power (Eds.), *The immersive internet: Reflections on the entangling of the virtual with society, politics and the economy* (pp. 125–137). Hampshire, UK: Palgrave Macmillan.

Clark, R. E. (1994). Media will never influence learning. *Educational Technology Research and Development, 42*(2), 21–29.

Consalvo, M., & Ess, C. (2011). *The handbook of internet studies* (Vol. 14). West Sussex, UK: Blackwell.

Dalgarno, B., & Lee, M. J. W. (2010). What are the learning affordances of 3-D virtual environments? *British Journal of Educational Technology, 41*(1), 10–32.

Dalgarno, B., Gregory, S., Carlson, L., Lee, M. J. W., & Tynan, B. (2013). *A systematic review and environmental analysis of the use of 3D immersive virtual worlds in Australian and New Zealand higher education institutions. Final report 2013.* www.researchgate.net/publication/279205705.

Dall'Alba, G., & Barnacle, R. (2005). Embodied knowing in online environments. *Educational Philosophy and Theory, 37*(5), 719–744.

de Freitas, S. (2008). *Serious virtual worlds: A scoping guide.* JISC e-Learning Programme, the Joint Information Systems Committee (JISC), UK.

Dudeney, G., & Ramsay, H. (2009). Overcoming the entry barriers to Second Life in higher education. In C. Wankel & J. Kingsley (Eds.), *Higher education in virtual worlds: Teaching and learning in Second Life* (pp. 11–28). Bingley, UK: Emerald.

Duncan, I., Miller, A., & Jiang, S. (2012). A taxonomy of virtual worlds usage in education. *British Journal of Educational Technology, 43*(6), 949–964.

Farley, H. (2011). Recent developments in virtual worlds and their potential impact on their use in higher education. In G. Williams, P. Statham, N. Brown & B. Cleland (Eds.), *Changing demands, changing directions. Proceedings of ascilite 2011* (pp. 381–385). Hobart, Tasmania: University of Tasmania.

Garrison, D. R., & Anderson, T. (2003). *E-learning in the 21st century: A framework for research and practice.* London: RoutledgeFalmer.

Gibson, J. (1979). *The ecological approach to human perception.* Boston, MA: Houghton Mifflin.

Gregory, S., Gregory, B., Reiners, T., Hillier, M., Lee, M. J. W., Jacka, L., ... Larson, I. (2013). Virtual worlds in Australian and New Zealand higher education: Remembering the past, understanding the present and imagining the future. In H. Carter, M. Gosper & J. Hedberg (Eds.), *Electric dreams. Proceedings of ascilite 2013* (pp. 312–324). Sydney: Macquarie University.

Haycock, K., & Kemp, J. W. (2008). Immersive learning environments in parallel universes: Learning through second life. *School Libraries Worldwide, 14*(2), 89–97.

Hedberg, J. G. (2011). Towards a disruptive pedagogy: Changing classroom practice with technologies and digital content. *Educational Media International, 48*(1), 1–16.

Heilig, M. (1992). Enter the experiential revolution. In L. Jacobson (Ed.), *Cyberarts: Exploring art and technology* (pp. 292–306). San Francisco, CA: Miller Freeman.

Helmer, J. (2007). *Second Life and virtual worlds.* Sheffield, UK: Learning Light Limited.

Henderson, M., Bellis, N., Cerovac, M., & Lancaster, G. (2013). Collaborative inquiry: Building pre-service teachers' capacity for ICT pedagogical integration. *Australian Educational Computing, 27*(3), 69–75.

Kariuki, D. (2017). OpenSim gains more land and active users. *Hypergrid Business.* [blog] www.hypergridbusiness.com/2017/06/opensim-gains-more-land-area-and-active-users/.

Kay, R. H. (2006). Evaluating strategies used to incorporate technology into pre-service education: A review of the literature. *Journal of Research on Technology in Education, 38*(4), 385–410.

Kelton, A. (2007). Second Life: Reaching into the virtual world for real-world learning. *ECAR Research Bulletin, 17.* Boulder, Colorado, ECAR. www.educause.edu/ir/library/pdf/ERB0717.pdf.

Kelton, A. (2008). Virtual Worlds? 'Outlook Good'. *Educause Review, 43*(5), 15–22.

Kirriemuir, J. (2012). *Zombies can't fly: The enduring world of the virtual.* Eduserv Foundation. www.silversprite.com/ss/wp-content/uploads/2014/10/snapshot-ten.pdf.

Kirriemuir, J. (2017). *Virtual world watch*. Eduserv Foundation www.silversprite. com/?page_id=353.

Knight, D. (1952). The analogues. *Astounding Science Fiction*, January, 36–45.

Koehler, M., & Mishra, P. (2009). What is technological pedagogical content knowledge (tpack)? *Contemporary Issues in Technology and Teacher Education, 9*(1), 60–70.

Laurillard, D., Oliver, M., Wasson, B., & Hoppe, U. (2009). Implementing technology-enhanced learning. In N. Balacheff, S. Ludvigsen, T. Jong, A. Lazonder & S. Barnes (Eds.), *Technology-enhanced learning* (pp. 289–306). Dordrecht: Springer.

Lawless, K. A., & Pellegrino, J. W. (2007). Professional development in integrating technology into teaching and learning: Knowns, unknowns, and ways to pursue better questions and answers. *Review of Educational Research, 77*(4), 575–614.

Newman, C., Farley, H., Gregory, S., Jacka, L., Scutter, S., & McDonald, M. (2013). Virtual worlds for learning: Done and dusted? In H. Carter, M. Gosper & J. Hedberg (Eds.), *Electric dreams. Proceedings of ascilite 2013* (pp. 622–626). Sydney: Macquarie University.

NMC. (2007). *The horizon report 2007 edition*. www.nmc.org/publication/nmc-horizon-report-2007-higher-ed-edition/.

Norman, D. A. (1988). *The psychology of everyday things*. New York: The Perseus Book Group.

OpenSimulator (2017). What is OpenSimulator? [wiki] http://opensimulator.org/wiki/Main_Page.

Savin-Baden, M. (2011). *A practical guide to using Second Life in higher education*. Berkshire, UK: McGraw-Hill.

Sutherland, I. (1965). The ultimate display. Paper presented at the IFIP. http://worrydream.com/refs/Sutherland%20-%20The%20Ultimate%20Display.pdf.

Sutherland, I. (1968). A head-mounted three dimensional display. Paper presented at the AFIPS. http://excelsior.biosci.ohio-state.edu/~carlson/history/.

Thomas, D., & Seely-Brown, J. (2009). Why virtual worlds can matter. *International Journal of Learning, 1*(1), 37–49.

Tice, S., & Jacobson, L. (1992). The art of building virtual realities. In L. Jacobson (Ed.), *Cyberarts: Exploring art and technology* (pp. 280–286). San Francisco, CA: Miller Freeman.

Warburton, S. (2009). Second Life in higher education: Assessing the potential for and the barriers to deploying virtual worlds in learning and teaching. *British Journal of Educational Technology, 40*(3), 414–426.

Wenger, E., White, N., & Smith, J. (2009). *Digital habitats: Stewarding technology for communities*. Portland, OR: CPsquare.

2 Disrupting norms

2.1 Introduction

The introduction of an innovative technology, like virtual worlds, into the conservative environment of education can be challenging because it has the capacity to disrupt the status quo. ITE faculty, students and K-12 teachers may not be willing or ready to change the way that they teach or to be challenged about their beliefs about how learning occurs. This is particularly in the context of a classroom, or in a subject area, where the 'teacher' has a lot of control over what and how they choose to teach. Therefore, what needs to occur for the introduction to be successful is for all the stakeholders to be open to be challenged and to be willing to take risks and make changes.

There is a growing culture of new understanding about the varied contexts in which learning takes place. Fullan (2013) identified a 'push-pull factor' in which the technologically enabled learning that happens outside of school is pulling students to learn outside of school and the increasingly bored and irrelevant environment inside school is pushing both the student and the teacher away. Thomas and Seely-Brown (2011) have called for a new culture of learning in which, as with Fullan, learning is occurring outside of the traditional institutions. Siemens' 'learning theory' of connectivism (Siemens, 2005) is gaining in popularity as ITE faculty see the need to update constructivist approaches to include the unavoidable outcomes of the use of networked technology. As early as 1970, Knowles questioned the term pedagogy when referring to the teaching of adults due to what he recognized as a different way of adults learning. The need to see that there are shifts in the way we learn is an important step in aligning the new technologies with the way that adults and children learn and the expectations for educational institutions.

2.2 A new culture of learning

For centuries, learning has occurred both outside and inside institutions and if the push-pull of technology in relation to education is to be avoided then a shift in our thinking about where learning occurs from the school to the learner needs to occur (Bentley, 2003; Fullan, 2013). Bentley (2003) concludes that the learner needs to be considered as 'an intelligent agent with the potential to learn from any, and all, of her encounters with the world around her' (p. 1). Once we do this then we must rethink what we expect to occur in a K-12 classroom environment and how the ITE faculty will prepare the student to teach in this environment.

The new culture of learning that Thomas and Seely-Brown (2011) propose is happening outside the confines of school or university; it 'takes place without books, without teachers, and without classrooms' (Chapter 2, para. 10). While this might sound like anarchy and the death of everything we know about schools and teaching, they propose that it does require boundaries but that there is freedom within those boundaries. Fundamental to their approach is that students' imaginations must be cultivated so that they are able to bridge the gap between the vast amount of accessible, networked information and the structured environment. There still needs to be guidance about how this might be achieved and one of the ways is that the classroom 'is replaced by learning environments in which digital media provide access to a rich source of information and play, and the processes that occur within those environments are integral to the results' (Chapter 2, para. 10).

According to Prensky (2010), the skills of a good teacher are still valuable in the digital classroom. He believes that the teacher needs to continue to do what they are already good at, such as 'asking good questions, providing context, ensuring rigor, and evaluating the quality of students' work' (p. 3). The technology provides the tools that help the teachers to do this work and to offer opportunities for the students to 'enhance their own learning' (p. 3). This 'partnering pedagogy' model (Prensky, 2010) is akin to a constructivist approach in which the teacher is the facilitator, who scaffolds learning. One area of criticism for this model is that it has led to a process designed to make learning easy for the student: too much scaffold. Davis and Sumara (2012) discuss the importance of 'effortful study' and that a teacher's role is to 'challenge, push, provoke, stretch, demand, make difficult' (p. 33). They believe that scaffolding has produced a sense that a student should not be able to fail and what it should be promoting is 'the sort of practice that happens at the limits of current competence, where there is a genuine likelihood of failure. However, lack of success here is not seen as demeaning or defeating. It is informative and transformative' (p. 33).

Introducing innovative technology into the teaching–learning environment can support new forms of learning. Beetham and Sharpe (2013) contend that technology has 'the potential to disrupt norms, challenge assumptions, innovate disciplines and professions' (p. 47). However, the majority of teachers continue to integrate technology by adding them into their current practices rather than considering new pedagogy that can be facilitated by technology. Ertmer and Ottenbreit-Leftwich (2010) suggest that teachers need help to 'understand how to use technology to facilitate meaningful learning' if they are 'to achieve the kinds of technology uses required for 21st-century teaching and learning' (p. 257). They stressed, 'despite increases in access and technology training, technology is not being used to support the kinds of instruction believed to be most powerful' (p. 257). A shift in thinking about the role of technology is required 'away from the notion that technology provides a supplemental teaching tool and assume, as with other professions, that technology is essential to successful performance outcomes (i.e., student learning)' (p. 256).

2.3 Disruptive innovations

There have been points in history when certain technologies have had the effect of being a disruptive technology or, what is now the preferred term, disruptive innovation (e.g. the printing press, the steam engine and the micro-computer). For an innovation to be disruptive it must at some point supersede what has come before. One contemporary example is that of digital photography. When first introduced, equipment was expensive and mostly used in professional settings (such as the media). As the technology became cheaper to produce and more people bought into the innovation, the previous technology of film and wet processing was superseded. Now most people can take photographs with their mobile phones and in some cases the purpose of photography has also changed. Our relationship with the camera has changed and with it our cultural understanding of what photography is.

The term disruptive technologies was first coined by Christensen (1997, 2000), who later called them disruptive innovation in order to highlight the importance of businesses recognizing that the value of an innovation may not at first be obvious or, initially, profitable. He suggests that 'products based on disruptive technologies are typically cheaper, simpler, smaller, and, frequently, more convenient to use' and that they initially do not perform as well as 'established products in mainstream markets. But they have other features that a few fringe (and generally new) customers value' (Christensen, 2000, Introduction, para. 21). Christensen et al. (2011) also applied the model of disruptive innovation to the K-12 classroom. One of the examples they use is that of online courses. In 2011, they described the exponential growth in enrolments on online courses by public school students. This growth demonstrates classic signs of disruption in which a shift occurs due to offering something that was not previously available. One of the key reasons for this success is that online courses were only competing with non-consumption; that is, the online course was better than no course at all.

Identifying whether technologies have been disruptive can help educators to realize whether the technology has made a difference to the learning experience and/or their pedagogical approach. Hedberg and Freebody (2007) stated that, while technology has been heavily invested in and implemented in the K-12 classrooms, 'no such disruptive technological innovation seems yet to have challenged traditional pedagogies' (p. 8). Hedberg (2011) cites interactive whiteboards (IWBs) as an example of a potentially disruptive technology that has not been realized due to the lack of application of learning approaches with these tools. He discusses three case studies that illustrate how the IWB can be motivating to students and that teachers can rethink their pedagogies. This shift was only able to occur after the teachers had been provided with professional development and with the inclusion of pre-made interactive learning objects in the IWB environment. The disruption occurred by the 'use of interactivity, speed of access, relevance, pictorial attributes and authenticity' (p. 15) that the learning objects brought to the technology.

Education might learn from business – in particular, the capacity for businesses to take risks and to not be afraid to fail. Christensen (2000) described five principles that he believes have led businesses to fail in terms of harnessing the potential of disruptive technologies, namely: resources, markets, applications, capabilities, and supply and demand. He states, 'the ultimate uses or applications for disruptive technologies are unknowable in advance. Failure is an intrinsic step toward success' (Chapter 2, para. 5). One of the ways that he reports that successful managers have harnessed this principle is that they 'planned to fail early and inexpensively in the search for the market for a disruptive technology. They found that their markets generally coalesced through an iterative process of trial, learning and trial again' (Chapter 2, para. 6). What we tend to see in education is a process of trial, learning and, if it is perceived to have 'failed', a move to something else, rather than a trial again.

The lesson that can be learnt from observing the patterns in the adoption of disruptive innovations is that they often at first appear to be of little value to current practices. It is not until the practices have changed in an almost synchronistic manner with the technology adoption that the type of use, usefulness and ease of use of the technology emerge as obvious and integrated parts of society and/or education.

An example of a disruptive innovation and the time in which it takes for the disruption to take place is that of email. First developed in 1971 when Ray Tomlinson connected his computer to his mailbox by using an @ symbol, email has moved through various phases of technology adoption before becoming the ubiquitous form that it is today. In the mid-1980s, the ARPA Net developed a system to make email more effective for its main users (being the military, students and academics). In 1998, the movie *You've Got Mail* positioned email in popular culture and individual consciousness. Fifteen years later, in 2013, there were nearly 3.9 billion email accounts (Radicati, 2013). Around the mid-1990s, educational researchers were presenting articles about email use in higher education, detailing the benefits and the barriers. More than forty years after Tomlinson first conceived of email, post offices have been forced to change their business practices as fewer people send print-based letters, email barely rates a mention in the academic literature and most individuals receive and send messages via their mobile phones through more than one account.

2.4 ITE can be the leaders

ITE has an important role to play in introducing, developing and supporting innovative pedagogy that disrupts the norm in order to meet the needs of twenty-first century learners. Technology needs to be integrated, discussed and modelled in ITE to influence the capacity of the ITE student to develop complex, authentic and student-centred pedagogy. Through doing this, ITE faculty and students can develop their digital literacy to include critique of technology and develop best practice to meet learning outcomes and needs.

There have been a number of studies that examine the way in which ITE programmes introduce the use of technology to their students and the way in which these approaches contribute to future classroom use (Beyerbach, Walsh & Vannatta, 2001; Fluck & Dowden, 2013; Gill & Dalgarno, 2008; Gill, Dalgarno & Carlson, 2015; Gulbahar, 2008; Hare, Howard & Pope, 2002; Kay, 2006; Mayo, Kajs & Tanguma, 2005). From these studies, some common themes have emerged. The most frequently reported aspect of technology integration is the barriers that affect the capacity of the ITE student and practising teachers when they attempt to implement technology in a classroom. Regardless of the type of technology (since they have changed over time) the barriers consistently cited are a lack of: (a) time, (b) information and (c) support. There have also been concerns raised by ITE students that during their university studies they are not provided with appropriate educational technology, computer facilities or knowledge about how to effectively integrate technology in their future classroom.

Beyerbach et al. (2001) in their study of ITE students at two US universities found that students wanted 'more learning about computer technology, sooner in their programmes' and that 'they needed a separate course in it, as well as needed to see it infused in all their education courses and field experiences' (p. 118). They reported that ITE programmes had sought to infuse technology use into their programmes, and studies such as Kay (2006) demonstrated that 'extensive time and money has been spent developing strategies and programs to help ITE students use technology effectively' (p. 392). However, Kay (2006) found that, despite these undertakings, there was scant evidence that these initiatives had been evaluated in relation to the actual effect that the introduction of technology to ITE students had on improving educational outcomes.

The most important factor in the effective implementation of technology in the classroom has been found to be the individual teacher; simply providing the technology hardware and software is not enough (Ertmer & Ottenbreit-Leftwich, 2013; Gulbahar, 2008; Painter, 2001; Twining, Raffaghelli, Albion & Knezek, 2013). The ability of the ITE student to conceptualize how they would integrate technology in their classrooms is a major barrier (Gulbahar, 2008) and they may not have been provided with this modelling in their ITE programme (Gill et al., 2015). This lack of self-efficacy, in integrating technology, may be driven by the fact that most ITE programmes teach computer skills, 'leaving the application in the classroom' to the ITE student's 'own initiative' (Mayo et al., 2005, p. 11). Ertmer and Ottenbreit-Leftwich (2013) suggest that to provide authentic technology-enabled learning the focus should be placed on the pedagogical rather than the technological and that this needs to be modelled and discussed in the ITE programmes. From Beyerbach et al. in 2001 to Ertmer and Ottenbreit-Leftwich some 12 years later, the way that technology is being 'taught' in ITE programmes has changed very little. What has changed is the actual technologies and what has not changed is the pedagogical approach to 'teaching' with and about technology.

There is often a gap between what ITE students are taught at university in technology-focused units, how the use of technology is modelled by university ITE faculty and what ITE students are then expected to do with technology when they are in primary and secondary school classrooms. In order for pedagogical transformation to occur, the ITE student needs to move beyond simplistic uses of technology in their classroom and provide opportunities for their students to use technology 'to research projects, analyse data, design products, and share their work within and beyond the classroom' (Twining et al., 2013, p. 429). A fundamental shift in the 'nature of the teacher-learner relationship' (Twining et al., 2013, p. 429) needs to occur. However, ITE students are often not given the opportunity to experience such pedagogical shifts themselves (as students), and many have not seen technology utilized in this way in their previous studies (at school or university) or in their practicum classrooms.

2.5 Virtual worlds in ITE

There has been a steady increase in the number of studies describing and analysing the use of virtual worlds in education and a growing body of knowledge specifically relating to the use of virtual worlds in ITE (Albion & McKeown, 2010; B. Gregory et al., 2011; S. Gregory et al., 2012, 2013; Kirriemuir, 2008, 2010; Messinger, Stroulia & Lyons, 2008; Moschini, 2010; Warburton, 2009). ITE is one of the most significant users of virtual worlds in higher education, particularly when investigating the impact on pedagogy. B. Gregory et al. (2011) highlighted this with an overview of virtual world use in ITE, indicating that 68 per cent of ITE programmes were using virtual worlds. Every year since 2010, the VWWG have produced a paper highlighting the use of virtual worlds by its members. Over this time, the discipline of education has ranked most highly as the area that is using virtual worlds and engaging with the academic community and research projects.

The implementation and impact of virtual worlds in ITE are often described through case studies, in which the author is also the course developer and teacher. In general, the ITE faculty have included some aspect of virtual world use with their ITE students and discuss how they did this and what the results were. This has resulted in a body of knowledge of ideas about ways to use virtual worlds in ITE programmes. The following section provides some examples from the literature.

Campbell (2009) taught an elective unit in Interactive Technologies that introduced students to virtual worlds and provided them with an opportunity to create their own virtual world teaching activity suitable for teaching in secondary schools. Typical comments from her students included 'I learnt so much about Second Life as I had never heard of it before. It brings up some great points of interest' and 'If this is where the future of education lies, I feel informed and confident about my ability to use it' (p. 14). Over half of the cohort expressed their willingness to use a virtual world in their future teaching. She observed that the virtual world 'is an exciting new area that, although still being researched by many, has a lot of scope, particularly in education and with students studying teaching' (p. 14).

S. Gregory and Tynan (2009) and S. Gregory and Masters (2010, 2012) worked for several years with a large cohort of ITE students integrating virtual worlds. One of their projects used role-play to explore de Bono's six thinking hats (S. Gregory & Masters, 2010, 2012). Each student avatar was assigned a coloured hat to wear and a topic for discussion. Using group chat, the students presented a point of view based on their hat colour, as represented in de Bono's model. Concurrently, students did the same role-play in the traditional on-campus tutorial setting. Some students participated in both the traditional and the Second Life sessions. S. Gregory and Tynan (2010) concluded that the:

> analysis of the results provides a positive reflection on Second Life as a teaching aid, particularly for novice users of Second Life, both academics and students, and discerns how it might be used as an alternative teaching aid in a variety of contexts.
>
> (S. Gregory & Masters, 2010, p. 12)

Zagami (2008) used virtual worlds as part of a creative arts and technology programme with primary ITE students. He found that the students using the virtual world could articulate their understanding of the creative arts syllabus equally and sometimes better than those who had not experienced the virtual world. Grenfell (2010, 2011) also used virtual worlds with creative arts ITE students to form authentic collaborative learning across disciplines, such as visual art education and public relations.

Cheong, Yun and Collins (2009) researched the 'potential power of Second Life as an environment for ITE students' teaching practice' (p. 1418). Their intention was to increase the students' access to teaching practice by providing a simulated environment in which they could 'experience an artificial teaching environment, practice skills without any harm to real students, and participate in problem solving by reflecting on their decisions and the effects they have had on students' (p. 1418). The study included 156 ITE students at Korea National University of Education, of which fifty-nine were asked to rate their experiences. The students' response was that the experience was beneficial and all of them satisfactorily completed their virtual world teaching practice. As a result, Cheong et al. (2009) concluded that using Second Life for teaching and learning with ITE students was a viable option and suggested 'more creative methods for providing these kinds of experiences' (p. 1421) should be developed in the future.

VirtualPREX was a research project funded by the Australian Office for Learning and Teaching (OLT) in 2011–2012 and it replicates Cheong et al.'s study on a larger scale. Five Australian and one international university utilized Second Life for ITE teacher professional experience role-play to 'test and develop a better range of professional skills and acquire confidence in, and more realistic awareness of, their skills before being placed in real-life classrooms' (S. Gregory et al., 2011, p. 491). They combined 'role-play in a realistic setting and Machinima for reflection and self, peer, formative and summative assessment [to] offer a significant, new option for supplementing ITE teacher learning' (S. Gregory & James, 2011, p. 7).

A similar project investigating the use of Second Life to develop ITE students' classroom practice was conducted at the University of Tasmania (Muir, Allen, Rayner & Cleland, 2013). In 2013, a pilot study was conducted in which eight ITE students undertook role-play activities. The role-play required the ITE students to behave as though they were school students with a range of diverse behaviours. After the role-play, the ITE students reflected on their experiences through group discussion. The intention was to provide the ITE student with authentic simulated experiences to help prepare them for their practicum. They found 'the use of a virtual classroom enabled real time role-play for geographically dispersed ITE students who did not have access to on-campus facilities or the opportunity to engage in collaborative reflection and peer discussion' (p. 13). They reported that Second Life had the potential to become a more efficient tool in education in the future when 'the provision of adequate time and resources and some of the limitations' (p. 14) were overcome.

Bower, Kennedy, Dalgarno and Lee (2011), described the *Blended Synchronous Learning Project* as 'identifying, characterizing and evaluating technology-enhanced ways of bringing together on-campus and geographically dispersed students and engaging them in media-rich collaborative learning experiences' (p. 150). To do this, they focused on three technologies – video conferencing, web conferencing and virtual worlds, analysing seven case studies of use across a range of universities. One of their conclusions was that the required level of bandwidth and technology are not yet available to create a ubiquitous experience of synchronous face-to-face and remote delivery, suggesting 'until that time, teachers will need to leverage the potentials of the available media-rich technologies to unite remote and face-to-face students, employing appropriate strategies in an attempt to mitigate or overcome the constraints' (Bower, Kenney, Dalgarno, Lee & Kennedy, 2013, p. 101).

What the literature to date has shown is that the discipline of education is a significant site for research into virtual worlds. One of the reasons for this may be that ITE faculty are concerned with preparing students to teach in classrooms of the future. As such, there is a pressing need to engage with technology that has the potential to challenge teaching practices and to align more closely with children's use of technology in their everyday lives. Albion (2008) suggested that the 'new generation of teachers and students are likely to be familiar with games and 3D online spaces as players and residents but may not be so familiar with the educational affordances that are on offer' (p. 1610). As such, there is an opportunity for ITE faculty to make those connections for the ITE student and to provide insight into the future classroom.

2.6 Virtual worlds in K-12 schools

The use of virtual worlds in K-12 schools is less well documented in the literature. Those that are reported have mostly been in collaboration with faculty at a university with K-12 implementation more visible in less 'academic' media, such as Twitter, Facebook or teachers' blog posts. However, a few key investigations have occurred with K-12 students using virtual worlds, including the highly successful work of teachers such as Sheehy and Gillespie (2017), who investigated the use of *World of Warcraft* (WoW) to engage students who were not finding success in the regular school system. They developed a resource to assist other teachers and to link the use of WoW to the Common Core Standards in the US (Gillespie & Lawson, 2013).

Barab is another educator who has worked extensively with K-12 teachers to design and implement the virtual world *Quest Atlantis (QA)*. For over a decade, QA has been utilized in school settings as a vehicle to harness game design features to engage students in deeper levels of thinking about authentic problems linked to the school curriculum. The outcomes witnessed in the use of QA has led to a 'rise in the belief that videogames are a powerful medium in which curriculum designers can create new worlds that invite youth to become scientists, doctors, writers, mathematicians, and the like' (Barab, Gresalfi & Ingram-Goble, 2010, p. 525). They describe the type of learning that occurs in QA as 'transformational play':

> The idea of transformational play draws upon the epistemological position that both knower and known constitute, and are constituted through, meaningful inquiry. Such a transactive view, as it relates to designing game-based curricula, requires not only recognizing the interrelations between the ways that person and situation can change one another, but also intentionally leveraging that realization to design for more powerful learning experiences.
>
> (p. 526)

The Schome project in the UK was founded on the idea that a group of faculty at the Open University, London could design an 'optimal educational system for the 21st century'; the premise being that 'there is widespread agreement that current education systems are failing to meet the needs of individuals and society in the 21st century' (Twining, 2009, p. 496). Schome was designed to mesh school and home (Sc-home) using a virtual world space in Teen Second Life. Teen Second Life allowed teenagers to access Second Life without being able to access adult areas, thus creating a safe space monitored by teachers (L. F. Johnson & Levine, 2008; N. Johnson, 2010). The Schome project ran from 2007 to 2008 with 149 gifted and talented youth given access to the pilot programme (Twining, 2007). While Schome had strong beginnings with many positive outcomes (Gillen, 2009, 2010; Gillen et al., 2009), the project did not continue due to a lack of ongoing funding (Gillen, personal correspondence, 2014).

In many public/government-funded K-12 schools, there are restrictions on the access to virtual worlds if they require connecting to a server that is external to the school (such as Second Life or other public grids). One of the ways to overcome this barrier is to use the stand-alone virtual world Sim-on-a-Stick (SoaS). Jacka and Booth (2013) documented the first successful implementation of SoaS in a public primary school in Australia. SoaS appears to be gaining in popularity through the dedicated online community; however, there has been no published academic literature about its use in education other than the aforementioned paper.

SoaS is based on OpenSimulator and there is scant literature on the use of OpenSimulator in the K-12 classroom. Independent schools (those not governed by the state or district governments) have been more able to host their own OpenSim environment and to access external virtual worlds. Independent schools using OpenSimulator and documenting their activities on school websites and blogs include: Northern Beaches Christian College (Sydney, Australia), China International Schools (Beijing, China), Gaelscoil Eoghain uí Thuairisc (Carlow, Ireland) and the Elizabeth Morrow School (New Jersey, USA). A group of NSW Department of Education schools have had access to OpenSimulator virtual worlds through collaboration with Macquarie University, as described by Cram, Hedberg, Lumkin and Eade (2010). With the development of the research project presented in this book, several regional NSW Department of Education schools have been able to utilize SoaS. These include: Coffs Harbour PS, Dunoon PS, Modanville PS, The Channon PS and Tyalla PS.

2.7 Conclusion

One of the drivers for implementing virtual worlds is the belief that norms need to be disrupted. Research has identified that traditional models of teaching are not supporting contemporary learning processes. However, the systems in which we believe that teaching is occurring (and in turn learning) are perpetuating the traditional models. The inclusion of a significantly different form of technology, one such as virtual worlds, presents an opportunity to create pedagogical practices that are attuned with the way that children are learning outside of school. If we can disrupt the norm through digital innovation that in turn becomes a disruptive innovation then we can hope to begin to see changes in the level of engagement that teachers, faculty and students will have for collectively coming together in traditional spaces for learning. There is potential for a blend to occur in which the physical space of the school or university campus links with the virtual space and provides significant shifts in the hierarchy between teacher and learner.

2.8 References

Albion, P. (2008). *3D online spaces for teacher education: Mapping the territory.* Paper presented at the Society for Information Technology & Teacher Education International Conference 2008, Las Vegas, Nevada, USA. www.editlib.org/p/27423.

Albion, P., & McKeown, L. (2010). *The seamless integration of Web3D technologies with university curricula to engage the changing student cohort* (CG7–488). Australian Learning and Teaching Council Report.

Barab, S. A., Gresalfi, M., & Ingram-Goble, A. (2010). Transformational play using games to position person, content, and context. *Educational Researcher, 39*(7), 525–536.

Beetham, H., & Sharpe, R. (2013). *Rethinking pedagogy for a digital age: Designing for 21st century learning.* Milton Park, UK: Routledge.

Bentley, T. (2003). *Learning beyond the classroom: Education for a changing world.* Milton Park, UK: Routledge.

Beyerbach, B., Walsh, C., & Vannatta, R. (2001). From teaching technology to using technology to enhance student learning: Preservice teachers' changing perceptions of technology infusion. *Journal of Technology and Teacher Education, 9*(1), 105–127.

Bower, M., Kennedy, G. E., Dalgarno, B., & Lee, M. J. (2011). Uniting on-campus and distributed learners through media-rich synchronous tools: A national project. In G. Williams, P. Statham, N. Brown & B. Cleland (Eds.), *Changing demands, changing directions. Proceedings of ascilite 2011* (pp. 150–155). Hobart, Tasmania: University of Tasmania.

Bower, M., Kenney, J., Dalgarno, B., Lee, M. J., & Kennedy, G. E. (2013). Blended synchronous learning: Patterns and principles for simultaneously engaging co-located and distributed learners. In H. Carter, M. Gosper & J. Hedberg (Eds.), *Electric dreams. Proceedings of ascilite 2013* (pp. 92–102). Sydney: Macquarie University.

Campbell, C. (2009). Learning in a different life: Pre-service education students using an online virtual world. *Journal of Virtual Worlds Research, 2*(1), 3–17.

Cheong, D. U., Yun, S., & Collins, C. (2009). Is Second Life effective for pre-service teachers' teaching practice? In I. Gibson, R. Weber, K. McFerrin, R. Carlsen & D. A. Willis (Eds.), *Proceedings of society for information technology & teacher education international conference 2009* (pp. 1418–1421). Chesapeake, VA: AACE.

Christensen, C. (1997). *The innovator's dilemma: When new technologies cause great firms to fail* (1st ed.). Boston: Harvard Business School Press.

Christensen, C. (2000). *The innovator's dilemma: When new technologies cause great firms to fail* (2nd ed.). Boston: Harvard Business School Press.

Christensen, C. M., Horn, M. B., & Johnson, C. W. (2011). *Disrupting class: How disruptive innovation will change the way the world learns.* New York: McGraw Hill.

Cram, A., Hedberg, J., Lumkin, K., & Eade, J. (2010). *Learning through design and construction in multi-user virtual environments: Opportunities, challenges and an emerging project.* Paper presented at the Global Learn Asia Pacific 2010, Penang, Malaysia. www.editlib.org/p/34325.

Davis, B., & Sumara, D. (2012). Fitting teacher education in/to/for an increasingly complex world. *Complicity: An International Journal of Complexity and Education, 9*(1), 30–40.

Ertmer, P. A., & Ottenbreit-Leftwich, A. T. (2010). Teacher technology change: How knowledge, confidence, beliefs, and culture intersect. *Journal of Research on Technology in Education, 42*(3), 255–284.

Ertmer, P. A., & Ottenbreit-Leftwich, A. (2013). Removing obstacles to the pedagogical changes required by Jonassen's vision of authentic technology-enabled learning. *Computers & Education, 64*, 175–182.

Fluck, A., & Dowden, T. (2013). On the cusp of change: Examining pre-service teachers' beliefs about ICT and envisioning the digital classroom of the future. *Journal of Computer Assisted Learning, 29*(1), 43–52.

Fullan, M. (2013). The new pedagogy: Students and teachers as learning partners. *LEARNing Landscapes, 6*(2), 23–29.

Gill, L., & Dalgarno, B. (2008). Influences on pre-service teachers' preparedness to use ICTs in the classroom. In R. Atkinson & C. McBeath (Eds.), *Hello! Where are you in the landscape of educational technology? Proceedings of ascilite 2008* (pp. 330–339). Melbourne, Australia: Deakin University.

Gill, L., Dalgarno, B., & Carlson, L. (2015). How does pre-service teacher preparedness to use ICTs for learning and teaching develop through their degree program? *Australian Journal of Teacher Education (Online), 40*(1), 36.

Gillen, J. (2009). Literacy practices in Schome Park: A virtual literacy ethnography. *Journal of Research in Reading, 32*(1), 57–74.

Gillen, J. (2010). New literacies in Schome Park. In A. Peachey (Ed.), *Researching learning in virtual worlds* (pp. 75–83). London: Springer.

Gillen, J., Twining, P., Ferguson, R., Butters, O., Clough, G., Gaved, M., ... Sheehy, K. (2009). A learning community for teens on a virtual island – The Schome Park Teen Second Life Pilot project. *eLearning Papers, 2009*(15).

Gillespie, L., & Lawson, C. (2013). *WoW in school: A hero's journey.* http://wowinschool.pbworks.com/f/WoWinSchool-A-Heros-Journey.pdf.

Gregory, B., Gregory, S., Wood, D., Masters, Y., Hillier, M., Stokes-Thompson, F., … Yusupova, A. (2011). How are Australian higher education institutions contributing to change through innovative teaching and learning in virtual worlds? In G. Williams, P. Statham, N. Brown & B. Cleland (Eds.), *Changing demands, changing directions. Proceedings of ascilite 2011* (pp. 475–490). Hobart, Tasmania: University of Tasmania.

Gregory, S., & James, R. (2011). Virtualprex: Open and distance learning for pre-service teachers. Expanding horizons – New approaches to open and distance learning. Presented at the 24th ICDE World Conference on Open & Distance Learning, Bali.

Gregory, S., & Masters, Y. (2010). *Six hats in Second Life: Enhancing preservice teacher learning in a virtual world.* Paper presented at the International Conference on Teaching and Learning with Technology 2010 (iCTLT), Singapore.

Gregory, S., & Masters, Y. (2012). Real thinking with virtual hats: A role-playing activity for pre-service teachers in Second Life. *Australasian Journal of Educational Technology, 28*(3), 420–440.

Gregory, S., & Tynan, B. (2009). Introducing Jass Easterman: My Second Life learning space. In R. J. Atkinson & C. McBeath (Eds.), *Same places, different spaces. Proceedings of ascilite 2009* (pp. 377–386). Auckland: The University of Auckland.

Gregory, S., Dalgarno, B., Campbell, M., Reiners, T., Knox, V., & Masters, Y. (2011). Changing directions through VirtualPREX: Engaging pre-service teachers in virtual professional experience. In G. Williams, P. Statham, N. Brown & B. Cleland (Eds.), *Changing demands, changing directions: Proceedings of the ascilite 2011 conference* (pp. 491–501). Hobart: University of Tasmania.

Gregory, S., Gregory, B., Hillier, M., Jacka, L., Farley, H., Stokes-Thompson, F., … Scutter, S. (2012). Sustaining the future through virtual worlds. In M. Brown, M. Hartnett & T. Stewart (Eds.), *Future challenges, sustainable futures. Proceedings of ascilite 2012* (pp. 361–368). Wellington: Massey University.

Gregory, S., Gregory, B., Reiners, T., Hillier, M., Lee, M. J. W., Jacka, L., … Larson, I. (2013). Virtual worlds in Australian and New Zealand higher education: Remembering the past, understanding the present and imagining the future. In H. Carter, M. Gosper & J. Hedberg (Eds.), *Electric dreams. Proceedings of ascilite 2013* (pp. 312–324). Sydney: Macquarie University.

Grenfell, J. (2010). *Teaching art education in blended immersive multiuser virtual and real world environments.* Paper presented at the South-East Pacific InSEA Regional Conference of Art Education, Melbourne, Australia.

Grenfell, J. (2011). *The best of all worlds: Immersive interfaces for art education teaching and learning in mixed reality virtual and real world environments.* Paper presented at the Canadian International Conference on Education CICE Toronto, Canada.

Gulbahar, Y. (2008). ICT usage in higher education: A case study on preservice teachers and instructors. *The Turkish Online Journal of Educational Technology, 7*(1), 32–37.

Hare, S., Howard, E., & Pope, M. (2002). Technology integration: Closing the gap between what preservice teachers are taught to do and what they can do. *Journal of Technology and Teacher Education, 10*(2), 191–203.

Hedberg, J. G. (2011). Towards a disruptive pedagogy: Changing classroom practice with technologies and digital content. *Educational Media International,* *48*(1), 1–16.

Hedberg, J., & Freebody, K. (2007). *Towards a disruptive pedagogy: Classroom practices that combine interactive whiteboards with TLF digital [online].* www. ndlrn.edu.au/verve/_resources/towards_a_disruptive_pedagogy_2007.pdf.

Jacka, L., & Booth, K. (2013). What about the firewall? Creating virtual worlds in a public primary school using Sim-on-a-Stick. *Australian Educational Computing, 27*(2), 13–17.

Johnson, L. F., & Levine, A. H. (2008). Virtual worlds: Inherently immersive, highly social learning spaces. *Theory Into Practice, 47*(2), 161–170.

Johnson, N. (2010). *Simply complexity: A clear guide to complexity theory.* Oxford: Oneworld publications.

Kay, R. H. (2006). Evaluating strategies used to incorporate technology into pre-service education: A review of the literature. *Journal of Research on Technology in Education, 38*(4), 385–410.

Kirriemuir, J. (2008). *Measuring the impact of Second Life for educational purposes: Responses and Second Life meeting transcript.* Eduserve foundation. www.silversprite.com/ss/wp-content/uploads/2014/10/Impact.pdf.

Kirriemuir, J. (2010). UK university and college technical support for Second Life developers and users. *Educational Research, 52*(2), 215–227.

Knowles, M. M. S. (1970). *The modern practice of adult education.* New York: Association Press.

Mayo, N. B., Kajs, L. T., & Tanguma, J. (2005). Longitudinal study of technology training to prepare future teachers. *Educational Research Quarterly, 29*(1), 3–15.

Messinger, P., Stroulia, E., & Lyons, K. (2008). A typology of virtual worlds: Historical overview and future directions. *Journal of Virtual Worlds Research, 1*(1), 2–18.

Moschini, E. (2010). The Second Life researcher toolkit: An exploration of inworld tools, methods and approaches for researching educational projects in Second Life. In A. Peachey (Ed.), *Researching learning in virtual worlds* (pp. 31–51). London: Springer.

Muir, T., Allen, J. M., Rayner, C. S., & Cleland, B. (2013). Preparing pre-service teachers for classroom practice in a virtual world: A pilot study using Second Life. *Journal of Interactive Media in Education [Online].* www-jime.open.ac.uk/articles/10.5334/2013-03/.

Painter, S. (2001). Issues in the observation and evaluation of technology integration in K-12 classrooms. *Journal of Computing in Education, 17*(4), 21–25.

Prensky, M. (2010). *Teaching digital natives: Partnering for real learning.* Thousand Oaks, CA: SAGE.

Radicati, S. (2013). *Email statistics report, 2013–2017.* www.radicati.com/wp/wp-content/uploads/2013/04/Email-Statistics-Report-2013-2017-Executive-Summary.pdf.

Sheehy, P., & Gillespie, L. (2017). World of Warcraft in schools. http://wowin-school.pbworks.com/.

Siemens, G. (2005). Connectivism: A learning theory for the digital age. *International Journal of Instructional Technology and Distance Learning, 2*(1), 3–10.

Thomas, D., & Seely-Brown, J. S. (2011). *A new culture of learning: Cultivating the imagination for a world of constant change.* Seattle, WA: CreateSpace.

Twining, P. (2007). *The schome-NAGTY Teen Second Life pilot final report: A summary of key findings and lessons learnt.* Milton Keynes: The Open University.

Twining, P. (2009). Exploring the educational potential of virtual worlds: Some reflections from the SPP. *British Journal of Educational Technology, 40*(3), 496–514.

Twining, P., Raffaghelli, J., Albion, P., & Knezek, D. (2013). Moving education into the digital age: The contribution of teachers' professional development. *Journal of Computer Assisted Learning, 29*(5), 426–437.

Warburton, S. (2009). Second Life in higher education: Assessing the potential for and the barriers to deploying virtual worlds in learning and teaching. *British Journal of Educational Technology, 40*(3), 414–426.

Zagami, J. (2008). Second Life as an arts education environment. In M. Docherty & D. Rosin (Eds.), *The art of serious play. The serious art of play. Conference proceedings of CreateWorld 2008* (pp. 3–7). Brisbane, Qld: Griffith University.

3   Making learning real

3.1 Introduction

The most significant affordance of virtual worlds for education is the capacity for the student to be immersed in an experience that simulates a 'real' experience. By so doing the student can be involved in exploration of content and ideas in ways that are not possible through traditional distance education or through some on-campus experiences. Activities that may have been too expensive or too dangerous can be explored. Students can revisit experiences alone or with others. Groups of external students can come together and interact with objects and artefacts as though they are in the same 3D space.

ITE students can experience being the learner and being the teacher as they interact with spaces knowing that they might also use them for their future teaching practice. As a teacher, they can utilize the capacity to create any resources they can imagine for their students to interact with, or they can offer the virtual world space as a creating space for their students. This opens the potential for them to be highly creative and expand their tool box of resources. It also offers the chance for them to shift their pedagogy into a student-centred space where students are in control of the path they take and the way they respond to concepts. The potential to make learning real is opened with a few skills and a willingness to experiment. The application of the virtual world fits with all disciplines and the ITE student begins to realize the potential through exposure to ideas and support during the early stages of introduction. This chapter describes four of the units in the ITE programme in which virtual worlds were explored – visual arts, science and technology, history and geography, and early childhood education.

3.2 Truly twenty-first century visual arts[1]

My K-12 teaching experience and background as an educator is in visual arts. As such, I imagined that virtual worlds could be utilized in several ways for a visual arts teacher. This included developing authentic art spaces in the virtual world as well as providing the virtual world as a place to create artwork. When I started using virtual worlds, visual art was a prominent feature of Second Life, with real-life galleries using the space and organizations such as the Australia Council for the Arts offering grants for artists to develop work in Second Life (Australia Council, 2010). The University of Western Australia has maintained an annual exhibition and 3D art prize since 2009, including a Machinima challenge. While their operations in Second Life have been scaled down recently, they continue to archive and support artistic practice in this space (UWA, 2017). One of the most well-known art spaces that linked very clearly to the traditional art curriculum was the Sistine Chapel that was recreated by the faculty at Vassar College, New York. This allowed anyone to visit the chapel and explore the artwork as though being there. Unfortunately, this space has been discontinued. This was also the fate of the space created by Ina Centaur called Primtings. She recreated well-known paintings by turning Second Life primitive objects into interactive 3D pieces, thus called Primtings. With these examples and experiences available, I chose to introduce my ITE visual art students to virtual worlds, assuming that they would be equally excited about this new creative space.

The unit in which the virtual world was used was the first of two units that they undertook in preparation for teaching visual arts in secondary school (elementary school). The students had not encountered the use of a virtual world in their higher education studies before, nor seen it used in a K-12 setting. Prior to the introduction of virtual worlds, the unit was delivered in weekly face-to-face tutorials over ten weeks. There were three different cohorts located at geographically separate campuses. Each cohort was studying the same unit with a different tutor and did not connect with each other. The new unit was developed to include meetings in the virtual world of Second Life; however, this was to be a small part of the whole experience and the level of interaction in the virtual world was four mandatory tutorial sessions and unlimited informal sessions whereby a student could nominate to meet with the tutor. The intention was to continue the use of Second Life in the next unit that the students would undertake. However, due to various circumstances the use of Second Life was discontinued.

Students undertook the following activities:

- participated in one two-hour virtual world workshop in an on-campus computer lab (n = 15)
- participated in four two-hour virtual world workshops conducted in Second Life (n = 16)

- attended field trips (n=6)
- attended individual meetings (n=5)
- created learning resources linked to virtual world experiences (n=2).

Prior to the first tutorial, the students were sent an email with instructions about how to open an account and make an avatar. They were asked to create an avatar before coming to the on-campus workshop. This was the only time that students from all three campuses would meet physically in an on-campus space. They were offered the opportunity to explore the virtual world before they came to the first tutorial but were advised that this was not mandatory as they would be stepped through the process during the tutorial. Over half of the students successfully created an avatar before coming to class and a third had accessed the virtual world. Only one student had prior experience in virtual worlds as a game player but had not used Second Life.

During the tutorial, the students were given access to the university's campus on Interaction Island and were asked to explore independently. The island offers lots of opportunities to interact with objects and looks similar to the physical campus. There were two expert users (myself and one other) available to assist the students and much of the time was spent helping the students to access audio and develop control of their avatar. The students who had previously visited the virtual world felt more able to explore other islands and started to interact with avatars from other places. After a period of independent exploration, the students were directed to an introductory space, outside of Interaction Island, which was designed to step new users through basic skills in using the virtual world.

3.2.1 Teaching and learning activities

The intention in the second tutorial was to use the virtual world to bring the student cohort together from separate physical locations but to retain the type of delivery of content that was familiar to them. As such, a 'traditional' lecture was presented that included a series of PowerPoint slides placed on flattened prim cubes that looked like large billboards. These boards were situated on a simulation of a grass-covered playing field, known as the Interaction Island sandbox. The students could walk around each of the slides that displayed text and images similar to a PowerPoint show (see Image 3.1). This was the first time that I had delivered content to a large group in a virtual world. The student feedback was that it made it more engaging as they were situated somewhere other than a lecture theatre; however, as the presenter I felt it was awkward and perhaps a bit distracting from the actual teaching. It was difficult to gauge the students'

Image 3.1 ITE visual arts students listen to a lecture on the Interaction Island oval.

interest or engagement during the teacher-directed parts of the virtual world sessions as they were mostly silent and unable to display some of the nuances that we are accustomed to in a face-to-face teaching situation.

Following the lecture, we walked (or flew) to the art space on the island where we interacted with a sculpture. From here I led a discussion that related to an aspect of the visual arts syllabus. We had an insightful conversation that included some avatar dance moves being displayed by one student and shared amongst the others. While this seemed to be off task, it lightened the mood in a way that felt acceptable and signalled to me the point at which the students were ready to move on to something else. We then teleported to the Vassar Island to explore the virtual Sistine Chapel. The students expressed that they could see the value for their future students in being able to visit a simulation like this.

The whole tutorial took approximately an hour and a half and presented a rich and varied experience that in the previous delivery of the unit would have been presented in a mostly teacher-directed lecture with some discussion and perhaps some resources linked from the Internet. In the virtual world, students could interact with each other by typing or having individual conversations without distracting the rest of the group or the main speaker. This is potentially a valuable exchange, both in terms of social interaction and in the sharing of ideas, particularly for students on small campuses, and can also help to establish a cohesive peer network across campuses.

Some students had been unable to attend the tutorial due to limited on-campus access so I conducted a repeat tutorial. I took this opportunity to try the same content but in a different space. I used one of the specifically designed spaces on Interaction Island that looks like a lecture theatre, with a data projector, screen, lectern and seats in rows (see Image 3.2). This space meant that the students were stationary, in their seats, and I stayed in one spot at the front of the room. At this early stage in our use of virtual worlds, this type of space provided an easier transition into using a virtual world but did little to change the way that this material was being delivered.

I was beginning to feel that we had progressed beyond our initial introduction to the virtual world and how it works. In the second session, I invited students to participate from the on-campus computer lab as well as in the virtual world. Two of the students attended in the lab, with most students now showing a preference for accessing the virtual world from home. For the tutorial, I had designed some activities based around the think, pair, share strategy that is commonly used in face-to-face classrooms. I posted a note card to the group that provided the initial instructions and would facilitate their engagement in the task without them

Image 3.2 ITE visual arts students listen to a lecture in one of the lecture theatres on Interaction Island.

needing to all arrive in the virtual world at the same time. I set up four painting easels at different parts of the sandbox so that each allocated group could congregate at different specified points. When clicked on, the easels then provided two inventory items – a note card with instructions and a note card with a step-by-step 'how to'. The note cards take on the same role as a handout or worksheet in the face-to-face classroom. The students were asked to create a note card that outlined the lesson ideas they had been developing as part of their first assessment task. They were then asked to talk to each other and share their lesson plan ideas. The final step was to make their own group note card with all the lesson ideas on. It was a simple replication of what we would do in a face-to-face setting in relation to sharing ideas.

The fourth and final session was designed to be similar to a practical face-to-face session with the use of the virtual world for creating artworks. The students based at one of the campuses were asked to attend in the computer lab to replicate how they might use a lab in their own teaching in a secondary school. The students at the other two campuses joined in the virtual world. As with the previous tutorial, the students were given instructions via a note card that they obtained when they logged on for the tutorial. The instructions asked them to import an image they had created and to place it on a flat surface. They were then asked to create an exhibition space that they could display their work in (see Image 3.3). The students who had been visiting the virtual world in their own time were at a

Image 3.3 ITE visual arts students create an exhibition space and place artwork on the walls.

stage where they could competently complete the tasks and develop ways to improve their building skills including interactive possibilities of the virtual world objects. The students were actively assisting each other and offering advice. As the facilitator of the group, I could assist students in the on-campus lab in a way that was familiar to me and worked well to improve the students' skills in relation to trouble-shooting particular issues, such as sound and avatar manoeuvrability.

3.2.2 Virtual field trips

The use of the virtual world to undertake field trips demonstrates easy access, multimodal representation, autonomy, interaction, interactivity and resources, as discussed by Lu (2008) as significant attributes of virtual worlds. It is of particular importance to tertiary and secondary students who live in regional areas as they are often unable to access art institutions as readily as their city counterparts. It also offers opportunities outside of cost restriction and personal inhibitions about interacting in a space such as an art gallery. Excursions may also include trips to places to gather material for use in artworks or to explore architecture such as the beach, rainforest, city and, in the case of the virtual world, Van Gogh's home, Ancient Rome or Frank Lloyd Wright's architecture. When visiting these locations, photographs (screen shots) can be taken and used for reporting on the excursion.

Students were given the opportunity to develop their own teaching practice and to explore the application of virtual worlds for the secondary school art classroom through the assessment tasks in the unit. The first assessment was a series of lesson plans based on any area of the syllabus. Two of the students chose to highlight the use of a virtual world as part of this task by incorporating the virtual artwork creation possibilities as one of the outcomes that a student might engage in. The second assessment offered three choices: plan an excursion, implement an information literacy task or develop a resource. Two students chose to develop a virtual excursion or field trip using Second Life.

One student created a virtual field trip that explored the Aeonia Art Gallery in Second Life. Following the previous tutorial model, she used note cards that the students would collect as they entered the world, giving them instructions to follow. The activities she asked the students to do included talking to the artist who is available in the virtual world in the form of her avatar. They were also directed to look at several pieces of artwork and to have discussions with their peers and the teacher. After they had done this, they would be making their own piece of work and writing a proposal to exhibit at the Aeonia Art Gallery. These activities are not dissimilar to what we might ask a student to do in a classroom. By using the virtual world, we overcome many of the issues associated with organizing a trip to a gallery, a talk with an artist and an exhibition. In the virtual world, a student may visit the gallery on numerous occasions, talk to a variety of artists and have the real opportunity of exhibiting in a public place.

Another student created a different type of experience for his students. His excursion into the virtual world was based around five different experiences that he called Art Trails. The students were asked to work in groups and follow a set of given instructions. The first Art Trail involved visiting the Primtings Museum where students were asked to locate several artworks. Each of the artworks in the Primtings Museum was based on an actual artwork, such as: *The Death of Marat* (by Jacques-Louis David), *The Elephant Celebs* (by Max Ernst) and *The Physical Impossibility of Death in the Mind of Someone Living* (by Damien Hirst). These works have been recreated so that an avatar can interact with them, as in *The Death of Marat*, where the avatar can actually lie in the bath.

The second Art Trail asked the students to visit VeGeTal PLaNeT and to identify three different digital works and answer a series of questions similar to an analysis that might be done using artworks in a book or in a gallery. The third Art Trail required students to visit Utopia Island 4 where they had to answer questions that were designed to activate thinking about a particular aspect of the visual arts syllabus. The fourth Art Trail was a game where students were required to get to the top of a tower on Utopia Island 1. The fifth and final Art Trail was designed to develop the students' building skills as they were asked to work in a team situation to build a sculpture on Interaction Island. By doing these last two Art Trails, the students were being asked to explore the virtual world and answer questions about whether this in itself might be considered art.

3.2.3 *Reflection*

The visual arts students had a mixed response to the inclusion of virtual worlds in their study programme. The ones who were the most resistant felt that they had been made to use the virtual world when they had expected to be in an on-campus class with a very small student–faculty ratio, in some cases as low as 2:1. They were understandably disgruntled that the mode of delivery was not what they had expected. However, it was a concern to me that they were studying to be teachers and yet they were unable to accept changes that were designed to open up their learning experience and their knowledge about innovations that they would be able to include in their future classrooms. Their responses revealed a lack of vision and flexibility, with comments such as: 'I would have preferred practical lessons, lessons where we discussed the assessments ... would have been much more useful than Second Life ... there's no way I can use Second Life in a real classroom'; 'I'm paying a lecturer to teach me what I need to know for my future, to have that lecturer deliver face-to-face classes. I have also found it extremely difficult to study the content online'; and 'Because the content was online and it was "work through at your own pace" there were no set deadlines despite the assignments. My other units got priority.' Another point of concern was that the students seemed unable to organize their own time, as reflected in the comments about the delivery mode:

> I found the 'flexible delivery' of the course very difficult. I enrolled in the unit expecting it to be on campus at fixed times. The way it was so 'flexible' made it incredibly difficult to juggle other family and work commitments.

There were several students who found the opportunity to be interesting and useful. They were grateful for the chance to look at teaching in a different way and to add the technology skills to their repertoire. Comments from these students included: '... it was refreshing and exciting to have the opportunity to learn through a virtual dimension, I commend the university for making this possible' and 'the tutor made herself available pretty much 24/7, this showed that she cared. ... She also offered valuable feedback.' These different perspectives reflect the place that the students were at in their journey as a learner and a teacher. Unfortunately, the comments made by the unhappiest students were heeded and the unit was not given the opportunity to be adapted and retried.

As the facilitator in the virtual world, it was difficult to make judgements about where the students were up to in the task and whether they needed intervention. When the students made note cards, they were working on their side of the computer interface and their avatar was stationary in the virtual world, giving the appearance that they were not doing anything. The students' avatars often appear to be just standing around and not engaged and this would normally be of concern to a teacher, and be judged based on body language. However, this would not be unusual if we were meeting in a LMS environment, such as Blackboard Collaborate or Adobe Connect. We would also not be able to 'see' what the students were doing, not meaning that they weren't doing what had been asked of them. This simply requires a shift in how the teacher interacts with the students and how we request feedback and interaction from the students.

The experience of the initial utilization of this educational technology confirms that virtual worlds have a role in visual arts education. There are a number of important and powerful aspects of virtual worlds that are motivators for further developing their use. First, virtual worlds are entirely created using all of the visual art elements and principles that underpin the visual arts curriculum. Second, students can continue using Second Life once they leave the university, including all of their inventory and the teaching resources that they have developed in-world. Third, working in a virtual world that has a large number of users and a healthy economy, which includes pre-built objects, the student can quickly develop environments and learning tools with little previous knowledge of building and scripting in a virtual world. Finally, through the use of the virtual world the secondary school teacher is endeavouring to link in with the experience of the young person who is already likely to be using virtual worlds as part of their play and social interaction.

3.3 Exploring science and sustainability

After the introduction of virtual worlds to visual arts students, I started looking for other faculty who might be interested in trying virtual worlds in their units. One of the first to volunteer was in the area of science and technology for the primary classroom. This unit was delivered on three campuses and, in the year that we used virtual worlds, had 225 students. For one of the workshops, and subsequent assessment items, students were asked to design and build a small model of a sustainable design project. Previously this resulted in students creating small-scale farms with solar panels and wind turbines constructed out of craft materials. The use of the virtual world meant that students could create their model in Second Life using shapes and textures that simulated a range of complex equipment and resources in relation to sustainable design (such as solar panels, wind turbines, wood, tin, vegetation and their own imagined versions of future sustainable design); thus, presenting a more authentic and potentially more transferable model of a sustainable design project. They could create and access objects that simulated sustainable design, experiment with their placement, proportion and functionality in a way that was not possible with the craft materials. They were also able to collaborate with other ITE faculty and students across the university campuses.

All of the students were asked if they would like to participate in the use of virtual worlds for these workshops, with no out-of-class time required; seventeen students volunteered. Twelve of the students participated in face-to-face workshops located in a computer lab at one of the campuses. The other five students were located externally. These five students attended separate workshops facilitated using Second Life. I met with them virtually while they worked together from the same physical location. All seventeen students attended a minimum of four hours of workshops over a two-week period.

Students undertook the following activities:

- designed and created a virtual world environment in response to an activity to assist students to understand the design process in relation to sustainable design principles (n = 17)
- participated in two two-hour virtual world workshops in an on-campus computer lab (n = 12)
- participated in two two-hour virtual world workshops conducted in Second Life (n = 5)
- presented their virtual world builds to the whole cohort (n = 4 groups).

Prior to the tutorials, a space on one of the university's Second Life islands was developed into an example of sustainable design, with the construction of a sustainable building (the eco house), which included simulations of solar panels, open spaces, rainwater tanks and vegetable gardens. The space was used as a meeting area in which tutorials were conducted with the students to discuss the concepts of design principles and sustainability.

3.3.1 Meeting in the eco house

The first tutorial commenced inside the eco house where there were a number of resources, such as: a slide show of images from the on-campus lecture showing sustainable design projects, a slide show of text outlining the design process, a diagram of the design process and two drawings by primary school children engaged in the design process. The first step was to orientate the students to the design process and foster an awareness of the need to engage in this process while designing their sustainable design project. Before they started to build, the students were required to develop a design statement and a design sketch. While seated in the eco house, the students collaboratively brainstormed their ideas about sustainable design, explored the science of sustainable building practices and discussed what they thought they might like to create. The use of the chat function, instead of speaking, allowed all students to type ideas simultaneously. The chat text was subsequently copied to a 'Google doc', which provided a record of the students' collective thoughts. The students were able to refine the design brief both 'in world' and at a later date on the 'Google doc'. Students were also provided with the opportunity to change their avatar's appearance, explore building through a game that I created and play with interactive objects (such as a bicycle). All of these activities assisted the students in developing confidence in the use of Second Life through exploration and play while maintaining a focus on the sustainable design experience. One of the differences between the classes conducted with this cohort and with the visual arts students was the use of an immersive space that replicated the task they were being asked to do and the 'feel' of the project (sustainability and design).

3.3.2 Building their designs

During the tutorials conducted in the second week, the students built their sustainable design project. They were given some instruction in basic building techniques (selecting and manipulating prims – the primitive shapes that all objects in Second Life are made from; choosing textures; purchasing objects in the market place). One of the groups spent extra time before and after the tutorial practising building and buying objects to add to the overall product. One of the affordances of Second Life is the ability to buy pre-made objects. The students who had limited building skills were able to create an environment that looked complete and demonstrated their use of the design process by choosing and placing pre-made objects such as rainwater tanks, solar panels, compost bins, vegetables, animals and buildings.

The four groups who created sustainable design projects in Second Life took full advantage of the affordances of the virtual world by creating round buildings with textures they imagined as potentially sustainable building materials of the future, such as solar cladding (walls made completely of solar panels). One group reflected in their design statement that:

> We took advantage of the Second Life environment and designed the building in the sky to maximize the density of housing and reduce our footprint. Our group discovered that building together required a great deal of problem solving and teamwork.

The designs included: a cylindrical building suspended in the sky with a vegetable patch and trees on top; one that hovered above the land to protect it from potential tsunamis with an interior designed for wheelchair access; and a 'kids' camp' situated beside the water that included animals and a solar swimming pool with a recycled water supply fed into a shower block. The most sophisticated design was a sustainable strawberry farm (see Image 3.4). This project was undertaken by a group who spent extra time on the build as they constructed a complete narrative around the project. They sourced materials from the Second Life market place that

Image 3.4 The completed strawberry farm in which strawberries could be grown
   with solar panels on the outside and climate controlled on the inside. A
   complete system of sustainable composting completes the design under-
   neath the building.

helped to enhance the 'believability' of their space. The use of the virtual
world made it possible to design and build a structure that the students (as
avatars) could walk into, around and experience. This provided a more
authentic aspect to both the creation and the evaluation of their projects.
The strawberry farm builders finalized their project with an invite to the
opening of the farm, in which the other students and faculty were asked to
attend and provide feedback.

3.3.3 Reflection

The literature suggests that most novice virtual world users are given a
significant amount of lead-time before they are expected to create objects
or environments. However, the experiences from the science and technology unit showed that the students were very quickly able to negotiate the
requirements of the virtual world and the building tools. All four groups

produced very creative work that demonstrated futuristic ideas about sustainable design. The students did not need extensive skill-based teaching to be able to construct objects that replicated their ideas about sustainable design. They engaged in experiential learning as they negotiated with the tools in Second Life to turn their sustainable design ideas into realistic simulations that could be interacted with and tested in the virtual world.

The group members who appeared to be the most successful in their level of building competence in Second Life and their own perceived level of success engaged in the planning, organizing, self-monitoring and self-evaluation to a very high level. While these students were required to participate in Second Life for only two two-hour sessions, this group chose to spend extra time, particularly in the planning phase. The comment below from a student in this group demonstrates their commitment to planning and hence utilizing the design process.

> We looked at where we would build, the impact on the immediate and wider environment, sustainable practices and any cultural or religious implications. By considering our design potential and the limitations associated with the actual build my team mates and I were ready to proceed to the producing phase.

This student also created a slide presentation where she discussed and reflected on the process and the value to her teaching practice. Another student chose to make a number of Machinimas (videos produced using screen-recording software) to demonstrate how he had made the design project as well as an introduction to the university's Second Life island. This shows that they were highly engaged in the process by putting extra time, which was not assessed, into the process.

The synchronous, persistent nature of Second Life allowed me to provide assistance and for the students to share ideas using an informal and collaborative approach across a number of locations. One of the students became highly skilled at building and mentored other students in Second Life, thus honing his teaching practice. A number of students from the Second Life groups commented on how they enjoyed this collaborative approach where they were able to get to know students who were on other campuses. In their design statement, one group reflected:

> We are all in agreement that it has been a fantastic experience and really emphasized the power of collaborative learning through all stages of the project. We had never worked together as a group before but quickly recognized our strengths, were willing to listen to each other and discuss strategies and prepared to put in the extra hours to

enable us to create the best possible result within the time frame. It was also discovered, through the learning journey, that this project's educational implications linked many of the KLAs.

3.4 Uncovering ideas about other cultures

One discipline within education that lends itself to the use of virtual worlds, as a predesigned space and as one in which students can create, is that of history and geography. Students studying to be primary school teachers, in Australia, are required to undertake studies in these discipline areas. I introduced virtual worlds to two different history/geography student cohorts over a two-year period. In the first year, students were given the option to use virtual worlds as part of an assignment and in the second year all students were required to create a resource using Second Life, SoaS or Minecraft.

All students in both years were provided with resources and opportunities to introduce them to virtual worlds for a primary class. These included group and individual workshops, a dedicated website and virtual world examples. They were provided with guidance to help orientate them to Second Life and information about how and why to use virtual worlds in K-6 education. Weekly hands-on workshops conducted in Second Life were offered for students to attend in their own time outside of regular tutorials. Students undertook the following activities:

- created an educational resource in Second Life for K-6 students (n = 30)
- created an educational resource in SoaS for K-6 students (n = 133)
- created an educational resource in Minecraft for K-6 students (n = 1)
- participated in one or more virtual world workshops in Second Life (n = 41)
- responded to surveys (n = 28)
- participated in a semi-structured interview (n = 3).

3.4.1 Creating a digital resource

In the first year, the ITE students enrolled in the history/geography unit were encouraged to use Second Life to create a digital resource for one of their assignments. Only three students chose this option, with all of them physically located over 100 km from me and the main ITE faculty. Due to this distance, they were supported in the building of their resource through one-on-one meetings with me in Second Life as I acted as the assistant to the students in the development of building skills and discussion of ideas suitable for virtual world learning spaces. Each of the students was allocated space above the main Education Research Island so they could build without visual distractions and without the need to remove pre-built buildings on the main part of the island.

The work produced by the three students in response to the assignment brief to develop a 'learning sequence and electronic resource' was of a very high standard in the application of skills for creating work in a virtual world and their ability to connect the virtual world experience to the K-6 classroom. One of the spaces built in Second Life has been used by a university in the USA to demonstrate the Indigenous struggle for equal rights in Australia.

They all started with different levels of experience. Student one was an exemplar student who by this stage had used Second Life in three of her other units of study, had implemented the use of virtual worlds in a classroom setting and had attended workshops and conferences in Second Life. Student two had used Second Life in the science and technology unit, described previously, in which she worked in a group to produce a 'sustainable design project'. Student three was a friend of the exemplar student who had encouraged her to work in Second Life and supported her with her project.

Student one built a large and fairly complex simulation of an African village to create a learning resource for a unit of work suitable for the topic 'Global Connections' (see Image 3.5). She imported two of the builds that her primary school children had created in SoaS and added her own features to some of the builds, such as a door to the mosque and a call to prayers. She bought objects from the Second Life market place and added them to the scene as she was a confident user of Second Life and the resources that could be obtained through the market place. Her focus was on 'World Food Aid' and she dressed her avatar with a pair of pants, a t-shirt and a hat to show the avatar as an aid worker. She found a sky box demo that created a feeling of being outdoors as it was placed above the island with a teleport point from the main island up to the space. She was initially concerned about using objects that other people had made. However, it became clear after some discussion that she was taking a curatorial role in bringing together objects to create a learning space. The assessment task was not grading her on her building skills and the unit of work was not 'teaching' students how to build in a virtual world but was 'teaching' students how they might use virtual worlds in a primary school setting.

Student two built a resource based on the theme of 'the family', with her families situated in an historical time in outback Australia (see Image 3.6). She used screen shots of images sourced from the Internet and placed

Image 3.5 An avatar dressed as a World Food Program worker stands amongst the simulated African village created by one of the ITE students.

Image 3.6 A simulation of colonial Australia, including animals, vegetables and a house created using prims and found images.

them on primitive boards in her virtual world space. These images represented people from the 1910s as they were dressed in costumes from that time. She also used images on the front of hollow primitive boxes constructed to represent houses. One of the house fronts included an image found of a 1910 rural dwelling on a real estate advertisement. Using these images created an extremely effective simulation of the time period without the student needing to develop sophisticated virtual world building skills to create buildings or people from the primitive shapes in Second Life. Furthermore, the use of photographs quickly creates a result that is pleasing to the creator, helping to alleviate some of the barriers that they may encounter when the building process starts to feel too difficult for them. The confidence that student two gained from including images and pre-made objects encouraged her to build some of her own objects and include simple scripts to display text and information note cards. I provided her with basic instructions about how to create note cards and scripts that she could use for a variety of objects. She went on to use virtual worlds in a subsequent unit and undertook a research project that introduced SoaS to a group of four primary school students.

Student three created a space that was museum-like, with posters made from flattened cube primitives and a few artefacts bought from the Second Life market place, to represent the freedom rides in Australia in the 1960s (see Image 3.7). She sourced black-and-white images from the event and included a 3D pool to represent a specific protest that occurred during these times; one in which Indigenous people were not being allowed in the public pool with the non-Indigenous people. When she began building she had no features that made her space significantly like a virtual world space; it lacked elements that were three-dimensional or interactive. We had many conversations about how

Image 3.7 The Freedom Rides were represented with a simulation of a swimming pool surrounded by images from the event.

to best utilize the 3D world as she grappled with why she would use virtual world in her teaching and how children might use her space. As she developed the space and thought about the potential, she started to add elements that made it more engaging for someone who was entering the space. Her work was later used by a US university who were also using virtual worlds in a similar discipline area and were interested in civil rights in Australia.

3.4.2 The next step

In the second year, all students (n = 161) were required to use Second Life or SoaS to create a digital resource. The same resources were provided as for the first year. However, a key motivator for the faculty to make virtual worlds mandatory was because one of the students from the previous cohort had gone on to use virtual worlds in a local primary school. She had become highly successful in working with primary school children using the virtual world and the faculty wanted to make sure that all the ITE students had some basic level of skill in this technology. To make this connection explicit to the current cohort, the exemplar student was invited to present two tutorials in Second Life and an on-campus lecture in which she brought two of the primary school children in to talk to the ITE students. All students were encouraged to attend one of the tutorials in Second Life but this was not mandatory and it was not programmed to occur within their designated tutorial times. Students were also given the option to sign up for a one-to-one workshop to help them work on their ideas and their building skills.

There were four main reasons that the task was made mandatory in the second year. They were:

1 It is powerful learning that is happening now and, for our students who are currently enrolled, to graduate without knowing what it is at all would be to under-equip them.
2 It provides an opportunity to put the students in a situation where they genuinely must take a risk with a learning process.
3 It is fun and different.
4 It offers a new way of working in a unit that was ready for a change.

As an introduction to the use of the virtual world, a presentation was given during an on-campus lecture, attended by the whole cohort of students. During the lecture, a Q and A was conducted in which the faculty asked me questions that they had and highlighted concerns they felt the students might have. A few weeks later, the on-campus tutorials included a screen recording of the WWI Poetry island from Second Life. This island allows the user to dress as a soldier or nurse and immerse themselves in the trenches of World War I. There are sound effects and visuals that facilitate the immersion of what it might have been like to be in the trenches during the war. As such, this provided an opportunity to illustrate how virtual worlds can help 'deliver' the history content that they would be teaching in a K-12 classroom. Throughout the semester, the students were invited to attend virtual world field trips to: the International Space Flight Museum, WWI Poetry, Australia Island, Exploratorium, Sploland, Eye of the Storm, OSU Medicine, Chinese Island, Religion Bazaar, Virtual MacBeth, Deakin Arts and the Sistine Chapel. All of these spaces provide outstanding examples of the potential of virtual worlds in education.

Students were encouraged to utilize SoaS as a virtual world that may be more acceptable in a classroom environment than worlds such as Second Life. The result was that they built work in SoaS and supplied only screen shots of the spaces as part of their assignments rather than submit the actual USB stick with the virtual world on. Some students used Second Life either because they did not have access to the correct operating system to run SoaS or they preferred Second Life. The students who used Second Life were allocated a small plot of land on the Education Research Island. There was an open invitation to request assistance when and if they needed it. I also 'dropped in' to Second Life to see if people needed help.

The students tended to create a museum-like environment in which they placed boards (flattened prims) with images on to represent the content area. The students who used Second Life accessed the market place to add in objects that they needed to source and make choices about as relevant to the topic. They worked in small groups and collaboratively designed areas that covered topics such as religions, cultures, celebrations and Indigenous perspectives. In Second Life, the students were allocated small sections of the island next to each other horizontally and vertically. This created an environment in which the students might be working simultaneously, similar to working in a studio space. They were also able to experience each other's work, which often does not occur when students produce work for assignments. This resulted in students developing a range of ideas for using virtual worlds with their future students (see Images 3.8 and 3.9).

3.4.3 Reflection

A survey was provided to students to ascertain to what extent the use of the virtual world had affected the pedagogical choices that they made. Twenty-four students responded to the survey. Twenty-two were female and two were male. Nine had used a virtual world before and fifteen had not. The types of virtual worlds they had previously used included SoaS, Second Life and games on PlayStation and Wii.

Image 3.8 Students were allocated space on a platform above the island. This bird's eye view shows eight of the building spaces.

Image 3.9 One of the builds addressed the theme of poverty through the use of 3D buildings and 2D images.

Students were asked to indicate how they felt before they started the assignment. Of the twenty-four responses, twelve expressed some concern about using the virtual world for their assignment, four were completely uninterested, five were interested and three were eager. The high level of concern was based partly on the students feeling that they normally did well in assignments and, due to their unfamiliarity with virtual worlds, felt they might be disadvantaged in this instance.

They also rated to what extent their perceptions of virtual worlds in education had changed while undertaking their assignment. Responses were fairly evenly distributed between those who indicated that their perceptions had not changed (n=9), those that were more neutral (n=7) and those that felt they had changed (n=8). Of the nine whose perceptions had not changed, five had remained the same because they stated they already could see the potential for virtual worlds. The other four either made no comment (n=1) or stated that they found it time consuming (n=2) or had too many issues with the programme (n=1). The seven responses that were more neutral all indicated that they could see how virtual worlds would be beneficial in the classroom. The students cited reasons such as student engagement (n=2), fun (n=1) and creativity (n=1). Of the eight respondents who indicated that their perceptions had changed, one had become more positive since his initial comments: 'It would be something beneficial, but it seems like a lot of work and without the knowledge too confusing. I wouldn't use it unless forced in the classroom.' The other seven responses ranged from stating that they could 'see what a valuable tool it can be in the classroom but before I wouldn't have looked at it at all' to believing 'virtual worlds should be implemented as a key component in most lessons'.

One of the questions asked about how the use of the virtual world influenced the type of lesson sequence that they designed for the assignment. Eleven responses indicated that the virtual world did not influence the design and that they simply added the virtual world in to the lesson sequence without fully utilizing the capacity of the virtual world. Of the eleven responses, two expressed that being required to include the virtual world had a negative effect on their lesson sequence. One of the students felt that they were 'more worried about getting that part of the assignment done as that was what everyone seemed to be focusing on as the main component', even though it was only a very small part of the actual assessment. The other nine responses indicated that the virtual world was added into their sequence after they had designed their lessons. One student stated that they 'made the lesson plans and after that decided what to do in the virtual world'. Another response showed that they were aware that they were not using the virtual world as effectively as they could as they 'used it in a very plain way with not much interaction involved'. They felt that they needed 'more time to play around with it and to become more confident with it first before I would utilize it frequently'.

There were nine responses that indicated that the use of the virtual world had influenced the design of their lesson sequence. Reasons given were that the virtual world provided engaging, stimulating, creative ways to enhance their lessons:

> I felt it was a great stimulus for the students and a great way to engage younger children. I aimed my unit of work at 7–9 year olds and Second Life gave me the opportunity to introduce a topic in an interesting way. I have a child this age and showed him what I made; he instantly engaged with the room and started telling me about it, which was exactly what I wanted.

Further feedback was requested to assist in future iterations of the use of virtual worlds. Students were asked about ways in which they believed the use of virtual worlds could be facilitated at the university. Their responses provided some insight into the factors that had affected their ability to utilize virtual worlds:

- being shown how to use the virtual world in workshops led by experienced tutors (n = 21)
- having more time (n = 15)
- having more resources (n = 3)
- better access to technology at university (n = 2)
- better access to technology at home (n = 1)
- if the virtual world was easier to use (n = 1)
- being provided with examples of use within K-6 settings (n = 1).

The students were asked to state what barriers might prevent them from using virtual worlds in their future teaching. Ten of the students indicated that they would need to increase their knowledge and confidence in using virtual worlds before they used it in the classroom. Other responses included if the school has the technological capabilities (n = 4), if other teachers are using it (n = 2) and if it becomes easier to use (n = 2).

Ten students chose to make an open response to virtual worlds in education. The comments were collated thematically and revealed that eight students had a mixed response, expressing both positive and negative comments, one made just a negative comment and one made just a positive comment. Nine of the responses attributed responsibility for their experience back to the actions of either the virtual world or the ITE faculty.

The negative responses to the virtual world included:

- the fact that they were part of an assignment (n=3)
- they were difficult to use (n=3)
- they required too much time (n=8)
- there wasn't enough support provided to teach them how to use it in a face-to-face workshop setting (n=4).

In contrast, one of the positive comments stated, 'I'm really glad I had the opportunity to interact with virtual worlds. The support from the lecturer was vital.'

Overall, the responses were similar to responses being given in other units and with other cohorts of students. Some students found the perceived demands in relation to time and technical requirements too burdensome and this was reflected in their perceptions of the usefulness of virtual worlds. The students who applied the virtual world to the educational setting in a way that enhanced the learning experience were more likely to respond in a positive way. As all students were required to use virtual worlds in the second iteration, there was added tension about the virtual world being included in assessment. At the outset, we felt that some of the students would be more reticent due to the assessment component. However, we also believed that this would provide extrinsic motivation that would facilitate the students to consider the use of virtual worlds. We decided that we were willing to accept negative student feedback to provide the students with an experience that they would not otherwise choose to take. Unfortunately, the student feedback resulted in virtual worlds not being made mandatory in the following iterations of the unit.

The students who took the option of using virtual worlds in the first year all had prior experience in either a hands-on building capacity (n=2) or through resources in a different unit (n=1). The high-stakes environment of producing work for an assignment put pressure on whether students were willing to take the risk. In the second year, the faculty decided to make all students use the virtual world. They had been motivated by a number of factors, not least of which was the experiences of the three students who did use the virtual world in the first year. Some extra resources and time were allocated to assist the students; however, the use of virtual worlds was still not fully integrated in a way that might have normalized the processes.

What was apparent from the responses to the mandatory use of virtual worlds was that some students were resentful that they were required to use an ICT that they were not confident with and that they felt they were going to be put in a situation that would result in poor grades. We were aware of the potential for negative responses and attempted to mitigate these by putting certain strategies in place. However, what we learnt from this was that it was impossible to cover all concerns and that many of the barriers were outside of our control, such as the students' own allocation of time to the task, their personal access to adequate technology and their willingness to overcome their own barriers.

3.5 Being an early childhood educator

Another unit also used Second Life as a mandatory part of the learning experience. This unit focused on preparing ITE students to work in early childhood education (birth to age five). One of the assignments had previously included a discussion of scenarios designed to start students thinking about how they would respond to certain situations in an Early Childhood Centre (ECC). By introducing Second Life as a tool to be used for this assignment, the students were able to actually role-play the scenario in an environment that simulated an ECC.

The students were provided with resources to help them become familiar with virtual worlds and to understand how virtual worlds could be used in the K-6 classroom. They were also given the option to attend workshops on campus and in the virtual world to familiarize themselves with how to use the virtual world. The level to which they engaged with the resources and workshops was voluntary. There were fifty-seven students enrolled in this unit, all of whom undertook the mandatory role-play activity. These students were studying to be early childhood teachers, who would most likely work with children from birth to age five. As such, the idea of the relevance of a virtual world for their future practice was challenging to most of the students.

In previous years, students had been given a written scenario that they would respond to by discussing it with their peers in a face-to-face tutorial. The faculty developed the scenarios based on situations that an early childhood educator might encounter in the workplace. Their peers gave feedback in relation to how effectively they responded to the scenarios. By using the virtual world, the students worked on a role-play scenario outlined by the faculty in which they acted out roles set within an ECC, designed and located in Second life. The role-plays were screen-recorded and played back during the on-campus tutorials, at which time their peers provided feedback.

Students undertook the following activities:

- responded to a scenario through role-play in an Early Childhood Centre (n = 57)
- participated in one two-hour virtual world workshop in an on-campus computer lab (n = 12)

- attended individualized group workshops (n = 45)
- responded to a survey (n = 15).

Resources were provided for the students, which included access to information and videos on the LMS and on a dedicated website for virtual worlds in education. I worked with students on campus to help them orientate to Second Life, create their avatar, navigate, and utilize voice and chat. When the students decided what props they wanted for their role-play, I helped them find these props and bring them into the virtual world space. A timetable was provided in which they could choose to meet with me to help them with any problems they might be having. I also provided weekly field trips that they were invited to attend. There was an 'open door' policy in terms of accessing help when and if they needed it. I attended all of the scenarios and recorded their role-plays for them. My level of assistance was designed to minimize the need for the students to learn too many technical skills and to concentrate on using the virtual world to convey their response to the scenario.

3.5.1 Role-play scenarios

The students were allocated a scenario that they would be required to turn into a script and role-play in Second Life. There were seven different scenarios, which included a variety of roles for the students to undertake. These ranged from being the Director of an Early Childhood Centre to a parent or a friend offering advice. The scenarios were presented to the students in a way that they would be required to decide how they would respond if put in that particular situation and they would write a script to help them tell that story. In Second Life, I provided a simulation of an Early Childhood Centre and assisted them in dressing their avatar appropriately and including any props they felt would enhance the experience.

One example of the scenario is:

> You are the Director of a 60-place long day care centre for 0–5 years. Children bring their own food to the service, and sit together at meal times. This enhances the development of their relationships with each other, and also gives them the opportunity to experience what other children eat. A parent has complained to you that one of your staff is not letting his child eat her chocolate bar. The parent explains that this is his choice to provide the food he wants for his daughter. Yet your policy says that the centre should advocate healthy food eating. How would you manage this, giving thought to the relationships between you and the parent, you and the staff member, the staff member and

the child? Also, what would you do about talking to the wider parent community?

The way in which the students responded to this type of scenario was to place their avatars in the ECC office with the Director sitting across the desk from the two parents. The skill level required to navigate in this way was very low. They used voice to talk to each other and interact from the script they had created. This was screen-recorded to be shown to other students at a later date. These recordings were posted to YouTube so that all the students could review what they had done. The intention was that the role-play would be critiqued by students and faculty as part of the learning experience. By creating the scenario in Second Life, and recording it, a wider circle of students and faculty could partake in the critique. The use of the virtual world to undertake the role-play provided an authentic experience for the students in which they embodied an avatar designed to appear as the actual 'character' would in real life and in a real-life setting. This level of 'realism' when undertaking role-plays is only possible in the virtual world. To replicate this in the physical world would require high levels of preparation in terms of costumes and setting. Another aspect to the use of Second Life was that students could use text chat if they felt that they were unable to use voice. In this iteration of the unit, there was a student who was deaf and the use of text chat helped facilitate her involvement in a way that had not been possible in the physical classroom (see Image 3.10).

Image 3.10 Three students perform a role-play as the Early Childhood Director and two parents. The text chat demonstrates the capacity to include text in the role-play situation in a virtual world.

3.5.2 *Reflection*

A survey was designed for the students to reflect on how the use of Second Life influenced their response and understanding of the early childhood scenario. Overall the responses to the survey could be divided between a positive response (n=4), negative response (n=6) and those who responded with both negative and positive comments (n=5).

Some of the ways that the students could see the benefit of using the virtual world was that it was a 'more interesting way to do the assignment' and they were 'able to visualize the scenario better'. The same student felt that it 'reduced their anxieties by not having to present information only in class'. In general, the positive responses recognized the potential for using role-play in the virtual world. They believed that it 'provided a more real-life context including the use of everyday speech and body placement'. One student stated that they were able to really put themselves in 'the shoes of my character in the scenario', which resulted in them feeling that they 'gained a deeper understanding by looking at it from this perspective'.

The students were given the opportunity to design the space in which they undertook the role-play and one comment was that this enhanced the experience by being able to 'add in your centre's philosophy, the early years learning framework, and other items that you feel will be good'. This allowed the students to undertake this task in a way that they would not normally be able to in a non-virtual world setting. The students could choose the clothes they would wear, the colour of the walls, the furniture, the toys and books, as well as the placement of these items.

One of the students also highlighted the convenience of being able to meet in Second Life to practise and perform the assignment task. She said 'all the members of our group were parents and so being able to access Second Life and work together later in the evening worked very well for us'.

The comments that conveyed a negative response reflected concerns that were either personal or technical. Those of a personal nature focused on the students' lack of confidence, fear of the unknown and the time it consumed or the lack of time they had to develop the skills. Other personal issues included the perception that Second Life was potentially addictive and that it had a tendency to display pornographic images.

The technology itself presented problems for some students who had difficulties because the computers at one of the campuses did not have the Second Life viewer installed or because they had a slow Internet connection at home. While this led to frustration, it did not stop the students from participating. They found ways to work around these barriers, such as using their own computers on campus or accessing Second Life when at a location with appropriate Internet connections. Due to the activity being linked to an assessment task, the level of frustration experienced was heightened and resulted in some students feeling disadvantaged.

One student found the task of writing content into a role-play conversation difficult and would have preferred to write an essay. This student would normally receive high grades when presenting an assignment in a more traditional mode and felt disadvantaged due to the technology requirements and expressed their frustration about 'having to spend time trying to get Second Life to work, and learning how to use it'. Another student gave advice about what they felt needed to happen in the future if virtual worlds were to be part of an assignment:

> If we were to undertake another assignment using virtual worlds, I think it would be advantageous to have class time to work together and learn how to navigate the virtual world and the avatars. Although Lisa was a great help, I think that more time would be necessary to fully understand how to use the world and then spend more time on doing the research and writing for the assignment.

This comment makes similar claims as those of students in other units; that of a lack of time. In general, the students felt that they were underprepared to fully understand and utilize virtual worlds for whatever task they were asked to use it with. The students were asked whether they would like the opportunity to use virtual worlds again in a university assignment. This question provided some insight into the response that the students had to virtual worlds, with approximately one third each stating that they would like to use virtual worlds again, they would not like to use it and that they might like to use it. The response indicates that there are clearly those who have a positive perception or experience of virtual worlds and those who have a negative one. The interesting group are those in the middle who are unsure. What this might reveal is that the students realize the potential for the use of virtual worlds and feel that with some of the barriers removed (their lack of skills, technical requirements, time to develop a better understanding) they would be willing to utilize virtual worlds in the future.

3.6 Conclusion

This chapter included four of the units in the ITE programme in which virtual worlds were explored – visual arts, science and technology, history and geography, and early childhood education. This represents a cross-section of the faculty and students who participated. The introduction of virtual worlds to these students revealed that there were barriers that restricted their capacity to engage with the technology and the learning outcomes. However, the students who were willing to overcome the barriers were able to experience learning in ways that they previously had not experienced. They were exposed to teaching and learning activities that challenged their ideas about what could be done in a K-12 classroom. The learning was made real through the types of activities that they were presented with and the way in which they conceptualized their own use of the environment for their teaching practice.

Note

1 Parts of this section are reproduced with kind permission of Australian Art Education. Previously published in Jacka, L. and Ellis, A. (2010) Virtual arts: Visual arts education in the virtual world of second life. *Australian Art Education, 33*(3), 125–139.

3.7 References

Australia Council (2010). In September, Australia Council for the Arts announced the recipients of its $20,000 artists residency in the 3-D online virtual world of Second Life. [Press Release] https://web.archive.org/web/20100311224257/www.australiacouncil.gov.au/the_arts/features/australias_first_second_life_arts_residency.

Jacka, L. & Ellis, A. (2010). Virtual arts: Visual arts education in the virtual world of second life. *Australian Art Education, 33*(3), 125–139.

Lu, L. (2008). Art CafÈ: A 3D virtual learning environment for art education. *Art Education, 61*(6), 48–53.

UWA (2017). Slartist@UWA Machinima Challenge – Joseph Nussbaum + Bryn Oh. [blog] http://uwainsl.blogspot.com.au/.

4 Perspectives

4.1 Introduction

ITE faculty design and facilitate experiences for students who have many different experiences and viewpoints. These students will, in their future practice, be working with students who are equally as diverse, and the environments will range from well-equipped to under-resourced. It is easy for educators to be excited by the latest technological innovation as it appears to present a way to engage students and provide new learning experiences. However, it is salient to acknowledge the warnings offered by theorists such as Selwyn (2014), who presents the view that it is important to resist an over-exaggerated enthusiasm for new technology.

4.2 Barriers

Barriers to the introduction and integration of technology is a common theme in education. Many studies have looked at what these barriers are and how to overcome them. However, they continue to be part of the technology innovation landscape and continue to cause problems for faculty who wish to introduce new technologies. ITE students report that they find the barriers start with a lack of skills in specific technologies before they can begin to think about the pedagogical implications and the benefits for learning.

From my study, five barriers were consistently cited by ITE students and faculty: time, access, the visceral response, perceptions related to K-12 students and negative feedback from students to faculty.

4.2.1 Time

Time was identified as a barrier by both ITE faculty and students. For the students, this was mostly based on their perceptions of the amount of time it would take them to be equipped to use the virtual world at a level they believed was necessary to integrate virtual worlds in a classroom. They also felt that the use of the virtual world would be time consuming in the K-12 classroom as their students would need to develop the skills and they would potentially be distracted from the teacher-designated tasks.

A lack of both perceived and real time is a genuine issue in universities for both ITE faculty and students. There has been a rise in what Concannon, Flynn and Campbell (2005) refer to as full-time part-time students. What this means is that students are enrolled in full-time study and have part-time jobs. The result is that students have less actual time to study and they develop skills in identifying and prioritizing what they need to study to pass their courses. This tactic is not new and was described in the 1970s by Miller and Parlett (1974) as being cue aware. Data from my research indicate that students were very cue aware as they spoke about how the virtual world appeared to be time consuming and that they were already busy completing other assignments.

A possible solution to the barrier of time could be to allocate more time within the set class times to introduce the students to the use of virtual worlds and then allocate a portion of time on a weekly basis, within the set tutorial times, to use the virtual world. This way the students would not feel that they had to dedicate extra time to learning to use the technology. However, such allocation of time would be only one step in changing the perceptions of the students. The units where time was allocated during the class still had students who reported that did not have enough time. It appeared that time was very much based on an individual's perceptions about what they valued in terms of time well spent.

Some students believed that talking about and learning to use virtual worlds was taking time away from learning how to teach in the physical classroom. Students found it difficult to conceptualize that they were not only learning about how to be a teacher in the present but also about teaching and learning in the future. They also lacked the experience to make connections between the type of learning experiences they were having in the virtual world and how this mirrored the type of teaching experiences they might design for the physical world.

ITE faculty also indicated that time was a barrier and they described themselves as time poor. One mentioned that if work time was allocated for them to explore the virtual world they would have been motivated to do so. Another stated that they had so many units that they were administering that they did not have time for anything extra or anything more interesting. Time, as a barrier for ITE faculty, was influenced by the level of intrinsic and/or extrinsic motivation (institutional support and/or professional rewards). In such circumstances, the level of motivation to pursue a new activity can result in the ITE faculty creating time in their schedule to engage in the activity (in this case, the use of virtual worlds) or choosing not to.

Extrinsic motivation was a significant barrier for the ITE faculty as they perceived that they needed a higher level of support from the institution for them to value the time that might be required to investigate the use of virtual worlds more fully than they did. They had support from me as I initiated and supported the actual use of the virtual world with the students. However, the discourse amongst their peers (other faculty) who were not using virtual worlds focused on the barriers and the negative comments from students. While there was a small amount of support from middle management, the use of virtual worlds was seen as peripheral to the core practices of the School of Education. ITE faculty are also cue aware as they prioritize the activities that they will gain the most reward from or that are the most pressing (such as the requirements of face-to-face teaching).

4.2.2 Access

Ease of access was another barrier cited by participants and was linked to the barrier of time. Given that the ITE faculty and students had trouble accessing the virtual world, a significant amount of time was spent as they made attempts to (a) connect to the virtual world (through Internet speed and viewer downloads) and (b) locate technology that could support the use of the virtual world either on campus or by upgrading their personal equipment. Many did not have computers with the level of graphics capability required to either run the virtual world or run the virtual world at a speed that facilitated a satisfactory experience. The ITE faculty and students who cited these barriers expressed that they became less motivated about the use of virtual worlds as their experience of access to adequate technology became an issue.

For some students lack of access was a barrier that they overcame. One student who became an exemplar user and teacher started her journey with virtual worlds without adequate access at home so she travelled to the university campus and used the computers that she had identified as suitable. Several other students reported that they had been motivated to get their own computer upgraded so they could use the virtual worlds. A few students on one of the campuses attended a virtual world tutorial while sitting in a hallway plugged into an Ethernet connection so they could access the virtual world at an appropriate speed and time.

To overcome the barrier of access, a higher level of support from the Computer Technology Services would need to occur. Future developments in the type of technology hardware and infrastructure required should consider not just what is being currently utilized but what might be used in the future. The Computer Technology Services should take advice from ITE faculty who are investigating innovative technology as well as providing leadership of future best practice and innovations. One issue that occurred in my research was the lack of support for computers that have high-end graphics capabilities. There were also restrictions on the use of particular ports in a bid to restrict students' over-use of websites such as YouTube. These restrictions resulted in limiting the ease of access that students experienced, particularly when first attempting to enter a virtual world. What became evident is that the few ITE faculty who were seeking to utilize technology outside of the current suite of applications needed to lobby university management and information technology services to support innovation, rather than the innovation being driven from the top down.

4.2.3 *The visceral response*

One of the barriers that is unique to virtual worlds relates to the immersive nature of the technology. No other technology currently in use in education requires the user to take the form of an avatar as they interact with their teachers and peers. The current capabilities of virtual worlds such as Second Life allow the user to embody a figure that has human features and can speak with their own voice. This experience was disorientating for some of the participants in my research. This is a visceral experience, as the individual makes a connection with their avatar that they embody as part of the process. This viscerality can lead to highly emotional responses in either a negative or a positive way. Emotional responses are intensely real and as such may lead to a complete rejection or inability to progress, especially if the experience may have been very unpleasant. In my research, the most commonly reported emotional response was the result of the participant encountering an unusual or what they perceived as a threatening situation. They may have been approached by an unknown avatar who asked them to engage in an act they were not comfortable with or they may have felt lost in a part of the virtual world with no way of getting to where they wanted to be. One of the ITE faculty stated that even though she wanted to engage with the virtual world she felt very 'uncomfortable being an avatar'.

The visceral capacity of virtual worlds can be a powerful tool in developing learning experiences. When it presents as a barrier, it needs addressing in a manner that does not inhibit the participants' ability to move beyond initial trepidation or negative experiences. As part of my research, support was provided for ITE faculty and students who experienced these barriers. A closed virtual world space was set up on the university island in Second Life and exact instructions were provided about how to get there. Synchronous contact was available to students through the LMS at the same time as facilitating entry into the virtual worlds to be able to communicate with any students who were lost. Possible scenarios that may occur and the capacity for the participant to simply exit the virtual world viewer, thus removing them from the situation, were described prior to their first entry into the virtual world. One-on-one sessions were also provided to help ITE faculty and students familiarize themselves with the skills required to navigate the space. The negative visceral experiences were the ones that generated a lot of discussion and negative discourse amongst ITE faculty and students to the point that they out-weighed the significantly higher proportion of participants who did not experience these problems.

A possible solution to the visceral barriers may be to identify the prior experiences and perceptions of ITE faculty and students well before the use of the virtual world in order to tailor specific entry stage experiences. There is an increasing number of ITE faculty and students who are familiar with being an avatar through digital games. Buddying them up with those who are less experienced may help to ease the process. Until the majority of ITE faculty and students are comfortable with what it feels like to interact in a computer-based environment through a 3D avatar, a structured introduction to immersion in virtual worlds is a prudent choice.

4.2.4 Perceptions of the K-12 classroom

A barrier that is unique to ITE students is the perception of the future problems they might encounter in a K-12 classroom. Students made comments that they were concerned that their future students would be distracted by the virtual world, lose face-to-face social skills or not have the technical skills or access to the technology. Furthermore, they had concerns about the virtual world as being unsafe, addictive and time consuming; all concerns that were heightened by the potential future use with children. These perceptions gave some of the students a reason not to investigate the use of virtual worlds further, while other students recognized that such problems were something they would need to overcome if and when they arose.

The perception about their future students not being on task was formulated from their own initial experience in which some of the students reported that they found it difficult to 'stay on task' when they were using the virtual world in the tutorial with a large number of students in the same virtual world space. In the tutorial, they had been presented with an unstructured virtual world activity – to explore the university island, to familiarize themselves with the virtual world and to begin to discuss how they might use it in the classroom. The students responded to the activity in a very playful manner; they spent time interacting with each other, changing their avatar shapes and clothes and exploring in-world games and artefacts. They perceived this playful behaviour as not doing 'serious work' and not 'being on task'. The response of the students reflects their perceptions of what they feel is appropriate behaviour in the classroom and what constitutes 'real' teaching and learning.

The students also cited cyber-safety and the addictive nature of virtual worlds as barriers. They transferred their perceptions and experiences of the virtual world of Second Life (highly social, avatar based and containing adult content) to assume that these issues would also exist in other virtual worlds used in K-12 classrooms. In an attempt to dispel these feelings of fear about virtual worlds, there was discussion at numerous points in the introduction of virtual worlds to reiterate that Second Life was not the virtual world that would be used with K-12 students and that it was being used in the university setting so as to learn about virtual worlds in a stable and accessible environment. Despite the discussion and resources provided to the students about the difference between Second Life and other virtual worlds more suitable for K-12 settings, the students continued to raise cyber-safety as an issue. One of the reasons for this may be that cyber-safety has been a major concern in K-12 educational settings for many years and as such is a key factor influencing the decisions about what type of technology to utilize in the classroom.

One of the ways in which to overcome the barrier of whether the virtual world is a safe environment for children would be to only use virtual worlds such as SoaS that do not require any access to a network and cannot be entered by people outside of the class. When the focus was shifted away from Second Life and towards activities that utilized SoaS, the student responses that indicated safety as an issue decreased.

The reason why some students moved beyond their perceived barriers about safety, addiction and what was real teaching and learning may have more to do with the mind-set of the individuals than the actual barriers. Dweck (2007) describes learners as having one of two mind-sets – the fixed mind-set and the growth mind-set. Those who have a fixed mind-set are unable to shift in their thinking as they believe that there are elements outside of their control that restrict their capacity to change. Those who have a growth mind-set are able to 'make a barrier an opportunity' and are driven by challenges. Recognizing that students come to certain situations with a pre-existing mind-set has implications for ITE faculty and for the students as future teachers. Dweck (2007) stressed that teachers enact their own mind-set in the classroom and, as such, impact on the mind-set of their students. The teacher thus has the capacity to perpetuate a fixed mind-set in their students and as such contribute to the extent to which the student is responsive to change.

4.2.5 Negative feedback

A barrier for the ITE faculty, when they were deciding whether to continue to use virtual worlds in their units, was the negative feedback some of them received from some students. As part of the university's system of feedback, each student is asked to respond to an online survey at the end of their units of study. The responses given by the students are used as part of the process of assessment of the ITE faculty performance and the result-ing number, based on the feedback, is used in various contexts, such as promotion within the university.

The negative feedback was not in the majority in any of the units; however, it was taken into consideration disproportionally to the positive feedback when ITE faculty described their virtual world teaching experi-ence. One faculty reported, 'Some loved it, then really loved it, some hated it, then loved it, some loved it, then hated it, some just hated it, then hated me.' This reflection shows an even number for and against yet the reasons given by this faculty for not making the virtual world mandatory in future iterations was the negative feedback. Other results of the negative feed-back were that in two of the units the use of virtual worlds was changed from mandatory to voluntary, and one removed the use altogether. The ITE faculty reported that this small amount of negative feedback was enough to make them reconsider whether they would utilize virtual worlds in their units. The reports by ITE faculty to other ITE faculty about the negative feedback had the follow-on effect of generating a negative dis-course and perpetuating negative perceptions by ITE faculty that had not yet tried virtual worlds.

It is not uncommon for only a small percentage of students to respond to the student feedback surveys. In units in which a new and challenging approach has been tried, students have a tendency to respond negatively and to let this be known through the feedback. This institutional barrier could be mitigated by creating a no-blame risk-taking policy in which ITE faculty who trial new technology are given the opportunity to defend the use and are supported to continue without fear of the student feedback impacting on their personal career options.

4.3 What do ITE students think?

Many of the barriers for ITE students and faculty come from their perceptions about virtual worlds. This leads them to question whether they are: (a) a learning tool, (b) appropriate for teaching and learning in K-12 education or (c) safe for children and adults. They display reluctance to enter the virtual world based on their perceptions rather than their experience. Many of the ITE students and faculty had very strong opinions about the relevance of virtual worlds for their practice.

During my research, I offered students the opportunity to consider virtual worlds either through actually entering the space or through readings, lectures, videos and discussions. They were then asked to give their opinion about whether they would use them, and whether they felt they were of value for teaching and learning. The largest data set came from students being asked to post to a blog in relation to their perceptions of virtual worlds for education. Prior to the blog post, they were asked to engage with content about virtual worlds that included a video, website and lecture streamed from within Second Life. They were not required to enter the world, but some did. Overall there were 311 responses collected over three years. This provides significant insight into what ITE students think about virtual worlds regardless of their actual immersion in them.

4.3.1 Themes

The initial 108 responses were analysed and four themes emerged. These themes were used to create a phases of realization model (see Jacka & Ellis, 2011). Each of the phases represented a point at which the student was describing their capacity to realize the potential to use virtual worlds in education. As the cycles progressed, the students' responses were mapped into each of the phases, resulting in an extended model to include five phases and being renamed to reflect more accurately what the phases were representing.

The phases of realization model was based on the analysis of the blog posts that judged the extent to which the student expressed their willingness to engage with virtual worlds as a technology for use in education.

The Pre-realization phase revealed that the students:

- could not see the benefit of using virtual worlds
- would not use virtual worlds.

The Realization phase revealed that the students:

- could see the benefit of using virtual worlds

- stated a number of barriers that would restrict their actual use of virtual worlds
- were unlikely to use virtual worlds
- demonstrated a conflict in perceived benefit versus barriers.

The Replication phase revealed that the students:

- could see the benefit of using virtual worlds
- were likely to use virtual worlds
- stated some barriers may still exist
- described the use of virtual worlds with traditional pedagogy.

The Reimagining phase revealed that the students:

- were excited about the use of virtual worlds
- were most likely to initiate the use of virtual worlds
- described the use of virtual worlds with innovative pedagogy
- stated minimal or no barriers. If barriers were discussed, solutions were offered.

In the earlier phases (Pre-realization and Realization), the barriers were the significant reason why the student would not contemplate the use of virtual worlds. In the later phases (Replication and Reimagining), the barriers were often acknowledged along with possible solutions, therefore presenting less of a reason for not progressing with their use of virtual worlds. To understand more about what factors were influencing the students' use and acceptance of virtual worlds in education, barriers were identified from the data. Four themes emerged which were then broken down into a further fifteen sub-themes.

Their personal experience was that they:

- were not on task in the tutorial
- felt uncomfortable or annoyed
- did not have the technical skills
- did not have access to the required level of technology.

They perceived that their future students would:

- not be on task
- lose face-to-face social skills
- not have the technical skills
- not have access to the required level of technology.

They perceived virtual worlds as:

* not safe
* addictive
* time consuming.

They perceived virtual worlds in the classroom as:

* needing to be linked to educational outcomes and objectives
* needing to be scaffolded
* taking up too much class time
* taking time away from non-computer activities.

A comparison across each of the iterations of implementation revealed that the focus of the barriers changed. In particular, the personal barriers lessened. Students' personal experience revealed concerns about being able to stay on task, their personal comfort levels in a virtual world, as well as the level of technical skills and access to technology that they had. A common concern expressed by students in the first iteration was that Second Life was 'too distracting' and they found it difficult to 'stay on task'. One student reflected that they personally 'find it difficult to concentrate' when they are at a computer as there is the 'temptation to check email or go on Facebook'. They felt that Second Life would add to the temptations and would encourage students 'to fool around and dance rather than do the tasks. They would want to customize their avatar, thus taking up valuable class time' (Student 34, Iteration 1). At this point, the student was linking their personal response to computer experiences, such as using Second Life, to what they imagined their future students would do. What heightened their concerns were their perceptions that the virtual world would disrupt learning rather than enhance it.

The students were presented with research that had been undertaken demonstrating positive results that virtual worlds can have when used in a K-12 classroom. However, the students who were at the earlier stage of the phases of realization made comments such as 'there was a suggestion that social skills may benefit from online games such as the Sims or World of Warcraft. To me this seems silly as social skills require interactions between people, face-to-face not through avatars' (Student 161, Iteration 2).

Only a small number of students believed that their future students would not have the required technical skills or access to the technology. This presented as a barrier as they felt that they would be required to teach their students how to use the virtual world. One student described it in terms of 'the extra technology skills and abilities the students would have to learn to undertake a lesson using virtual worlds could ultimately unravel the idea' (Student 104, Iteration 1). The follow-on barrier from feeling the need to teach the students how to use virtual worlds was the time they perceived this would require. In so doing, they felt that it 'would take up a lot of teaching time, for the students to be able to work their way around the virtual world, before they even are ready to think about what they are actually meant to be doing' (Student 37, Iteration 1). A further barrier in relation to time was the structure of the K-12 timetable in which the students perceived they would be required to deliver a certain amount of content. One student described their experience as:

> the school that I am currently doing practicum has 35-minute periods meaning that most of the lesson would be logging on to the virtual world and before they could even start the task it would be time to shut down the laptops again.
>
> (Student 278, Iteration 3)

Students whose curriculum area was primarily practical in nature (such as physical education, music and visual arts) consistently referred to what they believed to be an over-use of technology in the classroom and their desire not to add to it. One physical education student claimed 'students are on technology enough during the day and PDHPE is about living active lifestyles so involving them in activities where they are up and discussing the topic seems to be better than them typing away on the computer' (Student 278, Iteration 3). A visual arts student expressed that she could not 'see how having a virtual learning space within the visual arts classroom would be an improvement to the students' learning, especially in stage 4 and 5 where the majority of the class time is practical' (Student 348, Iteration 3). The visual art student displayed her belief that art practice is based in primarily non-technology based media. One of the music students also showed that their thinking about what constituted music practice was based in an approach that required musical performance to be experienced in real time and space; as they reflected, 'I am mindful of the fact that some things like witnessing and participating in live performance can only be experienced in real time and space' (Student 337, Iteration 3).

The students who had perceptions that virtual worlds did not have a role to play in their curriculum area were defining their approach to teaching based on their current experiences, either as a student or as an ITE student. As ITE students, they were understandably concerned with being able to link activities with the educational outcomes prescribed in state and national syllabus documents. One student from the curriculum area of English described how computer games had 'some value, as long as they are specifically adjusted to directly link to required outcomes' but that she could not see how 'creating a virtual world directly links to learning' (Student 166, Iteration 2). The use of digital games that are marketed specifically at education have become fairly common in classrooms; however, the use of a virtual world such as SoaS requires a higher level of conceptualization by the teacher to apply it to specific syllabus outcomes.

The level of confidence in the use of technology and specifically the use of virtual worlds was cited as one of the barriers. This also reflects the students' perceptions about how they are going to introduce technology in the classroom. If the student believes that the technology must be taught to the students by the teacher, then they need to rely on their personal skill level. This approach to the teaching–learning process is evident in the comment made by one of the students that 'online interaction requires plenty of scaffolding. This is particularly the case for students who do not have technology as a strength' (Student 26, Iteration 1). They elaborated that teachers themselves will need to be 'quite confident in the programme they are implementing in order for them to provide adequate scaffolding' (Student 26, Iteration 1).

A small number of the barriers were referred to as positive affordances in some instances of the data. These included: students being off-task (due to the engaging and entertaining nature of the virtual world), cyber-safety and a loss of social skills (due to not engaging face-to-face). For example, one student described how the virtual world could keep students engaged as it was 'a powerful tool that would motivate the students to stay on task' (Student 342, Iteration 3). Another student felt, in direct contradiction to some of the comments that cited concerns over control, that the virtual world allowed the teacher to 'introduce a controlled learning environment, where the parameters of the task are clear and specific, therefore allowing students to focus more directly on individual learning and development of critical thinking skills' (Student 287, Iteration 3). Some of the students described how cyber-safety could be taught by using the virtual world to role-play scenarios and to test boundaries in a safe environment.

One of the affordances of virtual worlds is the capacity to meet in the same space and engage in a shared experience. While this raised safety concerns for some students, others recognized that this presented a range of opportunities that many of their future students do not currently have. As one student observed:

> virtual worlds are opening up so many doors and opportunities for people to access educational tools first hand from all over the world. It eliminates the cost and travel time associated with going out and attending these events in person.
>
> (Student 65, Iteration 1)

Regardless of whether a student described factors that placed them in Pre-realization or Reimagining phases, there was consistent recognition that virtual worlds would be highly engaging for students in K-12 education. For those at the earlier stage of the phases, engagement was a distraction and at the higher end it was the main affordance. Many of the students reflected that they needed to become more familiar with virtual worlds and how to use them because of the interests of their future students and the need to engage them in learning.

The game-like features of the virtual worlds the students were introduced to and the association between games and virtual worlds meant that students were consistently referring to the virtual worlds as being fun. In some instances, the connection between fun and learning was seen as a negative in that being fun meant that they could not be learning something that should be serious. However, some students connected fun with learning and increasing the engagement of their future students, which would in turn foster a positive learning environment:

> The benefits of using virtual worlds for educational purposes include being able to target and develop particular skills, promoting teamwork and problem solving and getting students to use their initiative and be independent thinkers in order to create something ... and you can't forget how much awesome fun it would be for the students!
>
> (Student 155, Iteration 2)

The same student provided advice to teachers, saying 'it seems to me that what we as teachers need to do is think creatively and just be open to integrating new and unfamiliar methods into our pedagogy' (Student 155, Iteration 2). These types of comments highlighted that some students were able to link the need to utilize different pedagogy from that which they were currently being taught or observing in classrooms. They believed that, in order to fully utilize the virtual world in a way that transformed the learning experience for their future students, they would need to be open to change.

4.4 ITE faculty reflection

Most of the literature and research in virtual worlds is based on the work that the researcher has put in place and is undertaking as the primary faculty delivering their resources. In this research project, the faculty were novices in virtual worlds and were co-opted by me (as the researcher, designer and faculty). As such, I played a pivotal role in designing learning experiences, negotiating with faculty for time to implement activities and providing technical support for students and faculty. All of the faculty expressed that they would not have undertaken these activities without my support. The result was a lack of complete control over the allocated time spent in the delivery and the ongoing use of the virtual world. I believe that one of the most important aspects of integrating virtual worlds is the continued use of the space and a normalization of its use. Students and faculty have not always used PowerPoint, Word, email or the Internet and there were issues and barriers when these were first introduced. However, they are now ubiquitous in the working lives of students and faculty.

The ITE faculty were keen to experiment with virtual worlds but cautious about the level to which the virtual world activities were embedded in their units. They also felt time poor and not able to dedicate personal time to upskilling in the use of virtual worlds. The result was that I worked with the faculty to integrate virtual worlds in a small part of a variety of units. Before, during and after these activities, I discussed with the faculty how they felt about the use of virtual worlds and whether they would continue to use them.

One of the faculty believed that for students to be innovative in their use of technology they needed time, space, motivation and skills. They felt that students would not move beyond only doing what was required to pass the unit unless they had enough skills to stop them being stressed about using technology. The natural progression for a student being that they first work at what they need to do to pass the unit and, then, the more motivated ones move on to trying something more challenging. The result of the students progressing beyond basic requirements is that 'they don't know there is the potential to do it differently until they are in the process of using the technology'. This is a common conundrum for ITE faculty in relation to innovative technology integration. We must lead the way in terms of taking the risk to introduce the students to technology that they may be unfamiliar with and uncomfortable with for them to become familiar and in turn feel empowered to include the technology in their own teaching.

The sense of unease that can come with using innovative technology that presents the world in a different way was expressed by one of the faculty who described an uneasiness about the potential for virtual worlds to in some way shift or unravel their current philosophical position. They brought with them the belief that 'the things that we construct knowledge about, they're real, they're extent, they're mind independent and they're external to us'.

The primary motivation of the faculty for trying virtual worlds was that they could see the potential that virtual worlds could have for the K-12 teacher. However, they also wanted to (a) experiment with ways to be a co-learner with the students, (b) try a new technology that might be more challenging than other recent technological developments and (c) undertake a tutorial activity in a more authentic space.

Being immersed in the space and wanting to experience the space was vital to maintaining the interest of the faculty. One faculty remarked that the point at which they realized that virtual worlds offered a new learning experience was when they started coming to the workshops in Second Life while the students were learning how to build simple forms. During these sessions they observed, 'the learning process unfolds so that you get to see what the tool can actually do'.

> Last night at the workshop in Second Life I was standing off to the side watching while you had everyone down on the beach coaching them. There was a magical moment when, all of a sudden, boxes started to appear all over the sand. Classic.

At this point they had received positive feedback from the students:

> My email has overflowed with messages of excitement and thanks from students who were there at the workshop, and from students who didn't go, but have already heard about it from their mates! I feel a distinct groundswell coming on.

The faculty expressed a genuine understanding that the virtual world could provide a different pedagogical experience for them and the students. However, the barriers, including a lack of time, skill and experience with virtual worlds, meant that they struggled to know what to do with the virtual world. One faculty commented that it would 'be a terrible tragedy if all Second Life ended up being used for was an electronic replication of a tutorial'. While Second Life did not become an electronic replication of a tutorial, the real affordances were not realized. However, our expectations may have been too high for these initial experiences.

4.5 A critical lens

While it is important to investigate the integration of technology and the potential effect on current pedagogy, Selwyn (2014) warns that it is best to avoid presenting educational technologies in 'exaggeratedly enthusiastic terms' (Chapter 5, para. 11). Selwyn (2014) makes his point with the enthusiasm for games in education as an example. He believes that when faculty become enamoured by a particular technology, such as games in education, there is a tendency not to apply any level of critical evaluation.

By so doing he states that there are 'silences beneath this notion of games as an inherently "better" means of supporting educational engagement' (Chapter 5, para. 11). This can lead to following a path of integration of the technology before being informed of the actual pedagogical advantages over other forms of technology or non-technological approaches.

There has been a tendency for technology to be considered the panacea to improved educational outcomes for students and improved work practices for teachers. When a new technology emerges and becomes utilized in an educational context, the research into the use of the technology is often evaluated in terms of how to introduce the specific technology (including skills in use and barriers to overcome) without a critical evaluation of whether the inclusion adds anything to the current pedagogy (Selwyn, 2010). In ITE education, there is a need to create and maintain discourses that critically evaluate technologies rather than simply skilling the ITE faculty and students in the mechanics of how to use the technology.

There is a complexity to the adoption of technology in education, which must be considered, and developing a degree of distrust is warranted (Selwyn, 2014). This distrust, however, is more akin to developing a critical perspective, which is vital for all stakeholders to consider. Technology is pervasive in society and digital literacy is imperative in the twenty-first century but not all individuals are, or have been, willing adopters. Many people have had little choice but to become competent users in order to be part of society and the workplace.

Selwyn (2014) and Spring (2012) foreground the political nature of technology and reiterate the influence of the stakeholders involved when the use of educational technology is introduced, developed and supported. These perspectives are particularly important in the context of academic research. As Selwyn (2014) writes, an 'orthodoxy appears to have developed in most parts of the world that digital technologies are an integral and inevitable feature of "modern" forms of education, and therefore require little or no discussion' (Chapter 1, para. 3). The lack of discussion and the tendency to introduce technology through teaching about how to use the technology, rather than why to use the technology, has led to many new technologies failing to live up to expectations.

4.6 Conclusion

The lens through which the ITE students and faculty looked at virtual worlds had a significant impact on their willingness to integrate them into their toolbox of educational resources. The scepticism that Selwyn suggests that we approach new technologies with is well founded. However,

ITE students and faculty need to be careful to not use this lens as a reason not to dig deeper and critically analyse the affordances and potential. Barriers are evident at all levels of professional practice and whether we choose to overcome them will depend on the motivation to achieve the end goal. Repeatedly the same barriers have emerged in the introduction and integration of technology in education. Virtual worlds present some new barriers but perhaps not surprisingly many similar ones to technologies that were once innovative. Finding ways to overcome these barriers lies in a united approach to the adoption of innovation in education supported by the institution, infrastructure and society.

4.7 References

Concannon, F., Flynn, A., & Campbell, M. (2005). What campus-based students think about the quality and benefits of e-learning. *British Journal of Educational Technology, 36*(3), 501–512.

Dweck, C. (2007). *Mindset: The new psychology of success*. New York: Ballantine.

Jacka, L., & Ellis, A. (2011). *Developing a checklist for evaluating virtual worlds for use in education*. Paper presented at the Global Learn Asia Pacific 2011, Melbourne, Australia. www.editlib.org/p/37375.

Miller, C. M., & Parlett, M. (1974). *Up to the mark: A study of the examination game*. Guildford: SRHE.

Selwyn, N. (2010). Looking beyond learning: Notes towards the critical study of educational technology. *Journal of Computer Assisted Learning, 26*(1), 65–73.

Selwyn, N. (2014). *Distrusting educational technology: Critical questions for changing times*. New York: Routledge.

Spring, J. (2012). *Education networks: Power, wealth, cyberspace, and the digital mind*. New York: Routledge.

Conclusion

What we learnt

The work that I have been doing in introducing virtual worlds to ITE faculty and students has resulted in a significant number of people becoming aware of the potential of this innovative technology to influence their practice. Not all faculty or students used virtual worlds and not all of them agreed that it had a role to play. However, the data collected over the research revealed that attitudes were changing.

There was consistency in the variety of perceptions, motivations and barriers. The main motivation for the students was that their future students would be highly engaged by using virtual worlds in the classroom. They also indicated that the affordances of virtual worlds would provide opportunities for their future students to: develop collaboration skills; be active participants in the teaching–learning process; have an increased capacity to express themselves by being an avatar; and develop lifelong learning skills. They also acknowledged that the virtual world provided the potential to undertake experiences that were too expensive, too dangerous or not possible to do in the non-virtual world.

Students were able to describe, to varying degrees, reasons why they felt that virtual worlds would be useful in K-12 education. However, being able to describe the usefulness of virtual worlds for K-12 education did not always translate to the students personally feeling that they would use virtual worlds. A number of factors needed to align for students to believe that they would actually be able to implement the use of virtual worlds.

Reasons they gave for considering the use of virtual worlds were opportunities to:

- develop student-centred experiences
- engage students
- develop teamwork

- promote problem solving, initiative and independent thinking
- collaborate with other schools.

There were concerns and barriers based on their perceptions before and after experiencing the virtual world. These concerns included that they:

- perceived they weren't staying on task due to the distracting nature of the environment
- perceived they would experience technical issues
- perceived that using the virtual world would be time consuming
- experienced feelings of annoyance
- experienced feelings of discomfort
- experienced technical issues.

They also perceived that their future students would:

- lose face-to-face social skills
- not be on task
- not have the technical skills
- not have access to adequate technology.

These perceived issues had the potential to be barriers for students when they were considering whether to invest personal time into exploring virtual worlds. The students who expressed these barriers, in some instances, described them as restricting their ability to use virtual worlds in the classroom, but some students described them as a barrier that would not restrict them, as they would find the means to overcome them.

There were a number of factors that influenced why more students did not use virtual worlds when they were given the option as part of an assessment. This included that they felt there were easier and quicker technology options with which to complete these tasks. The students who did use virtual worlds expressed that they had perceived that using virtual worlds would be challenging, but that the level of challenge was one of the motivating factors. Some of them felt that, in hindsight, what they had actually done in the virtual world did not represent what they could have done.

In the one unit in which all students were required to use a virtual world, a mixed level of approach and satisfaction was achieved. The majority replicated traditional teaching practices with images or text placed in the space to be interacted with by looking at or reading. Almost one third responded by creating and describing ways that their future students would use the virtual world as a way to learn more about a theme through immersion in a simulated environment or to build their own representations of knowledge about a theme through building in the virtual world. This level of response was despite there being only a small amount of technical support provided.

The ITE students who were most successful with the virtual world activities and assignments were not the students who might appear to be the most technologically savvy but the students who were able to conceptualize the task as one that was designed to help them develop learning activities for their future students. One of the faculty observed that the 'young students that think they are techy because they are on Facebook does not mean they will automatically be good at constructing a worthy learning space in Second Life'.

Overall, the students' responses from all of the units indicated that they were influenced by a complex interplay of their perceptions as well as their experiences. Sometimes their initial perceptions were so negative that they chose not to engage in an immersive experience. These pre-existing perceptions were developed either through their prior experiences, as a small number of students were virtual world game players, or through second-hand information, such as media reports or stories from friends or colleagues. After being introduced to virtual worlds as part of their units of study, their perceptions may have changed. This seemed largely dependent on whether they did have an immersive virtual world experience and whether they perceived the experience as positive or negative.

One student became very experienced in her use of virtual worlds as she developed increasingly sophisticated approaches in both building techniques and her pedagogy. The success that she had with her creation of virtual world environments was a critical factor in motivating the ITE faculty to include virtual worlds in their units, as it demonstrated the real potential for virtual worlds in K-12 education.

What I learnt was that certain aspects of the delivery were successful and could be built upon for future iterations. This included offering the use of virtual worlds as another way that students could respond to assessment tasks; thus, accommodating students who are highly motivated or who have an interest in emerging technologies. If we wish to require all students to utilize virtual worlds, a more concerted approach towards scaffolding the skills and providing explicit models of how virtual worlds could be used should be provided as a mandatory part of the unit. Furthermore, the design of the assessment criteria may need to have a change in focus so that the students feel that the effort they put in to learning how to use the virtual world is also given some recognition. At this point in time, the initial 'learning how to use the technology' barrier appears to be high when there is limited time allocation to delivery of courses.

Recommendations

Based on the responses, factors and level of readiness, the following recommendations are made to assist the integration of virtual worlds in teaching and learning. A framework is proposed that, if put into place, will optimize the introduction, support and development of virtual worlds to assist in the development and use of innovative pedagogy.

University

Universities' level of infrastructure and management is a key contributor in the process of promoting innovative pedagogy. The introduction of virtual worlds in university programmes needs to be aligned with ITE faculty training, information technology services and a reconceptualization of the pedagogy and learning design (O'Reilly, Ellis, & Jacka, 2014). While virtual worlds can be used in a university without the complete support of information technology services, if a minimum level of support is provided then the innovators amongst the faculty are more able to grow the use of virtual worlds.

Virtual worlds have specific information technology requirements so that the user experience is as close to seamless as possible and that the user is able to experience a 'suspension of disbelief' (Dede, 2009). With low-end graphics and slow processing speeds, the experience can lead the user to feel that the experience is less than satisfactory when they are in a situation that is designed for learning. In all universities, the faculty and students are restricted by the information technology services that are provided to them. In many cases, the information technology services are also restricted by what the university management determine is appropriate in terms of support and level of technology based on a variety of factors, including budgetary constraints and overall philosophical goals of the university. If the university is motivated to provide and develop innovative technology, then the commitment to fund innovation may be less of an issue.

School of education

The discipline of education, within a university, is the only sector in which the act of teaching is that which is being taught. ITE faculty are engaged in the act of teaching adults about teaching children and as such they are required to both teach appropriately for adult learners and model practices that are appropriate for children. Lunenberg and Korthagen (2003) describe this: 'teacher educators not only teach a subject (teaching), but

Table C.1 Recommendations for the management, information technology services and professional development services in a university to introduce, support and develop virtual worlds at a small, medium and full scale

Small to medium scale	Full scale
Management	*Management*
• Support voluntary use of virtual worlds across the university	• Mandate the use of virtual worlds across the university
• Acknowledge work undertaken in the use of virtual worlds	• Acknowledge innovative work undertaken in the use of virtual worlds through the inclusion of case studies in reports, newsletters, media releases and awards
• Provide funding to pilot the development of a virtual world environment	• Generate positive discourse through personal acknowledgements, conversations and directives
	• Fund the development of virtual worlds
Information technology services	*Information technology services*
• Some computers on campus set with adequate specifications	• All computers on campus (including fixed and mobile) set with the specifications to run a variety of virtual worlds
• Set ports so that proprietary virtual worlds such as Second Life can be accessed	• Set up an OpenSim environment hosted by the university
• All computers to be updated six-monthly with the latest version of virtual world applications	• Faculty have mobile devices capable of running virtual world viewers in order to access away from campus
• Information technology staff to have a basic knowledge of virtual world viewers and platforms	• Configure all ports to allow access by faculty and students using their university or personal computers/devices
	• Update all computers/devices when required by the virtual world viewers
	• Information technology staff to take a leadership role in relation to providing advice on current trends in virtual worlds
	• Information technology staff able to provide expert help to troubleshoot technical, hardware and virtual world viewer problems
Professional development services	*Professional development services*
• Training provided for faculty that includes technical skills and pedagogy	• Actively promote the importance of the development of technical skills and pedagogy
• Support networking between faculty who are using virtual worlds	• Have professional development staff who are knowledgeable in virtual worlds and are using them in their own practice
• Develop models of best practice	

Table C.2 Recommendations for the head of school, faculty and students in an ITE programme to introduce, support and develop virtual worlds at a small, medium and full scale

Small to medium scale	Full scale
Head of school • Provide professional development to faculty who are interested in virtual worlds that includes allocating time for them to develop skills and resources • Promote the work of faculty who are using virtual worlds • Encourage a positive discourse about the use of virtual worlds • Fund the development of a virtual world environment in one course	• Increase the level of the recommendations in 'small to medium' and: • Encourage and support research using virtual worlds • Provide recognition to the use of virtual worlds as part of the mission of the school • Take a leadership role in the use of virtual worlds and in the process of change • Use the virtual world environment for meetings and discussion amongst faculty
Faculty • Design small virtual world learning experiences • Join collaborative networks to discuss virtual world learning experiences • Generate a positive discourse by promoting the work of other virtual world faculty • Encourage the students to become involved in virtual world use in their courses • Provide students with opportunities to use virtual worlds regardless of the set task	• Design more complex virtual world learning experiences as part of a team of designers • Join collaborative networks to discuss, critique and design virtual world learning experiences • Mentor other faculty and students • Conduct research and present work at conferences, and in books and journals • Encourage and support students to become experts
Students • Attend sessions run by faculty to introduce them to virtual worlds • Practise virtual world skills in workshops and at other times • Be open to trying to utilize virtual worlds • Design virtual world learning environments on a small scale in virtual worlds such as Second Life and SoaS	• Develop skills in virtual worlds beyond any basic expectations driven by assessment • Join networks of innovative K-12 teachers using virtual worlds • Design virtual world learning environments on a larger scale in virtual worlds such as Second Life and SoaS • Implement virtual worlds in K-12 schools • Mentor faculty and students in the use of virtual worlds

are also role models for teaching. In this respect their profession is different from, for example, doctors teaching medicine' (p. 32).

Developing models of pedagogy that do not necessarily mirror the models that ITE students observe when in a K-12 classroom can be challenging and confronting for ITE faculty. In order for the accepted integration of innovative technology to be successful, ITE faculty need to create an environment in which ITE students are willing to explore new pedagogy. This will only happen with a systematic and concerted endeavour by all levels of staff within a university.

ITE faculty need to be supported by their university as well as being intrinsically motivated about the use of virtual worlds. Once they are using virtual worlds with their students, they can utilize pedagogy that facilitates the best learning outcomes and model best practice. The students need a high level of extrinsic motivation and the removal of barriers in order to fully understand and utilize virtual worlds, both in their studies and as practising teachers. The main extrinsic motivators need to be rewards that recognize the effort required by them in using and designing virtual world environments. These would most commonly be in the form of assessment tasks and the affiliated grades and grade weightings.

Where we are going

As I was undertaking this research, my practice began to move into the use of virtual worlds in K-6 education as I created opportunities to work in the school environment to create classroom examples of use for the ITE students and faculty. What became vitally important was the ability to present a strong case to the ITE students about why they should take time to overcome barriers to learn how to best use virtual worlds for their future practice. A significant influencing factor to the shift in use of virtual worlds was the identification that the virtual worlds, as a technology, worked in the classroom setting, that children were engaged using the technology and that the classroom teacher was equally enlivened by the inclusion of the technology in their practice.

The research presented in this book represents a phase in which the seeds were sown for the use of virtual worlds in education across several subject areas and with a significant number of ITE students. However, only a small number of these students extended their use of virtual worlds in their studies and into the K-12 classroom. A question that remains unanswered is to what extent the introduction of virtual worlds in the ITE programme has impacted on the future teaching practices of the students in this research. A longitudinal research project that maps the use of virtual worlds over an extended period of time and into the classroom would offer insight into the learning potential of virtual worlds in both ITE and K-12. This would require a longitudinal study that follows the students who have been introduced to virtual worlds in their professional practice to observe in what way their approach to their pedagogy develops and changes.

Six faculty were directly included in this research; however, a number of other faculty were also exposed to the use of virtual worlds as tutors within the units. Anecdotal evidence implies that the discourse generated by all faculty had an impact on the willingness of the ITE students to utilize virtual worlds, particularly when the conversations reinforced the ITE students' negative perceptions. The main faculty also referred to their inability to control what the tutors said in tutorials and their awareness that tutor comments may provide mixed messages to the students. Further research could include observations of tutors in relation to the way they present new ideas. A comparison between tutors in similar contexts could be undertaken to determine whether certain attitudes were influencing the ITE students in a manner that was counterproductive to the motivations of the unit designer. Interventions could be provided to evaluate what processes need to be put in place to generate a discourse that critiques the use of virtual worlds without being critical.

Ideally, a fully integrated and supported introduction of virtual worlds in a way that highlights and promotes their potential would help to shift the current perceptions of virtual worlds. This would need to include support for faculty and students in the development of resources to work in the virtual world. There would need to be buy-in from all stakeholders, in a sustainable manner. The ITE students would need to be supported and encouraged to implement virtual worlds in a K-12 context and to collaboratively develop resources that further extend the use of virtual worlds. A community of practice would be created in which innovative ideas were supported, developed and rewarded. By creating this context and then collecting research data, the element that appeared to be most lacking from this research would be evident; the continuity of use of virtual worlds in a manner that allowed the ITE student and faculty to build on their initial perceptions, experiences and skills.

This research has concentrated on the virtual worlds of Second Life and Sim-on-a-Stick and their use in a university context. During this research, differences were observed in the way in which children and K-12 teachers responded to virtual worlds compared to the way in which the university ITE faculty and students responded. This may be explained due to the pre-existing perceptions and experiences that K-12 children bring to virtual worlds. It is likely that K-12 children's views are related to, and derived from, game playing and, as such, a high level of engagement. They are less concerned with the educational value of the virtual world than ITE faculty or students may be. Further research would be valuable to systematically investigate the introduction of virtual worlds in the K-12 context, evaluating responses and the factors that influence the K-12 teachers and children. The results of such research would usefully inform ITE programmes and provide empirical evidence about the capacity for virtual worlds to have a positive impact on K-12 education. The aim of this research would be to provide recommendations and examples that could be used to guide future practice and to influence the ITE students to adopt virtual worlds while studying to fully utilize virtual worlds in their future teaching practice.

Conclusion

The practical examples and insights presented in this book support the theory that there are significant complexities that affect any innovation in an educational setting. Throughout the implementation, there were early adopters who have spread the use of virtual worlds into the school community. However, the full integration of the virtual worlds at the Regional University in Australia was not sustainable and in-roads continue to be sought out. We are at a point where the use of technologies that facilitate a cross-over between what we perceive as real (or physical) and what we perceive as virtual (or not real) is becoming more accepted and less of a novelty. As more people use 3D virtual worlds in their everyday lives and as more positive publicity is generated, the educational community will begin to feel less nervous about fully integrating these tools and allowing faculty, students and teachers flexibility to realize pedagogy that is not wedded to traditional models of learning. We can make learning real; we just need the spirit to let it happen.

References

Dede, C. (2009). Immersive interfaces for engagement and learning. *Science, 323*(5910), 66–69.

Lunenberg, M., & Korthagen, F. A. (2003). Teacher educators and student-directed learning. *Teaching and Teacher Education, 19*(1), 29–44.

O'Reilly, M., Ellis, A., & Jacka, L. (2014). Immersing ourselves in professional learning. In S. Gregory, M. J. W. Lee, B. Dalgarno, & B. Tynan (Eds.), *Virtual worlds in online and distance education*. New York: NOVA Science.

Index

Adobe Connect 53
Aeonia Art Gallery in Second Life 51
affordances 17–20, 56, 91; of
  educational technology 18, 38; of
  virtual worlds 19, 86, 92
Albion, P. 38
Ancient Rome 51
art spaces 46, 48
Art Trails (virtual world experiences) 52
arts 33, 36, 45–6, 48–52, 54, 56, 62, 64,
  85, 90; creative 36; visual 45–6, 73,
  85
artworks 46, 50–2
Australia and New Zealand Virtual
  Worlds Working Group 13–14, 35
Australia Council for the Arts 21, 46

Barab, S. A. 38
barriers 1, 3–4, 15, 17, 21–5, 33–4, 69,
  72–86, 88–94, 98; generalized 4;
  identifying 21, 24; institutional 81; for
  ITE students and faculties 82;
  perceived 80; personal 84; visceral 79
Bentley, T. 30
Beyerbach, B. 34
Bitner, N. 4
Bitner, J. 4
Blackboard Collaborate 14, 53
Bower, M. 18, 37

Campbell, C. 35, 76
campuses 9, 47, 50, 58, 72, 77; separate
  46; small 48; university 54
Carlson, L. 6, 23
Centaur, Ina 46
Channon, The PS 39
Cheong, D. U. 36

children 15–16, 29, 40, 63, 69–70,
  79–80, 82, 95, 98–100; grooming of
  15; and K-12 teachers 100; primary
  school 55, 60, 63; younger 67
classrooms 2, 25, 29–30, 33–5, 37–8,
  52, 66–7, 80–1, 84–7, 92–3; digital
  30; physical 71, 76; practices 37;
  settings 15, 60, 98
Club Penguin 15
Coffs Harbour PS 39
collaborative learning 58; authentic 36;
  effective 18; media-rich 37
Computer Technology Services 77–8
computers 13–14, 19, 23, 33, 72–3,
  77–8, 84–5, 96
Consalvo, M. 25
content 4, 14, 45, 47, 49, 53, 73, 82, 85;
  educational 15; user-created 16
Cuban, L. 2–3
curriculum assessment and new media 9
cyber-safety 80, 86

Dalgarno, B. 6, 18, 23, 25, 37
Davis, B. 10, 30
de Freitas, S. 21
Death of Marat, The 52
design 14, 16–17, 38, 54–8, 66–7, 72,
  76, 94, 97; learning 5, 95; process
  18, 55–6, 58; statements 55–6, 58
development 14, 18, 24–5, 39, 59, 70,
  77, 86, 95–7, 99; of building skills
  59; of education in virtual worlds 25;
  of technical skills and pedagogy 89,
  96; of virtual reality and virtual
  worlds 14, 96
digital resources 59, 63
Dudeney, G. 22–3

Dunoon PS 39
Dweck, C. 80

e-learning platforms 7
Early Childhood Centres 69–70
ECAR 21; *see also* EDUCAUSE
    Center for Applied Research
ECC 69–70; *see also* Early Childhood
    Centres
education 1–3, 7–10, 14–16, 23, 25,
    29–30, 32–3, 35–7, 82–3, 89–91; early
    childhood 45, 69, 73; physical 85
education systems 26, 39
educational changes 2
educational outcomes 18, 34, 84–5, 90
educational researchers 5, 17, 33
educational settings 5, 24, 68, 80, 100
educational technology 9, 18, 34, 54,
    89–90
EDUCAUSE Center for Applied
    Research 21
Ellis, A. 95
emails 33, 47, 84, 88–9
environments 9, 13–15, 17, 29–30, 54,
    56–8, 64, 69, 74–5, 93; computer-
    simulated 14; games 21–2; in-world
    13, 16; virtual 7, 16, 18
Ernst, Max 52
Ertmer, P. A. 4, 31, 34
Ess, C. 25

face-to-face 9, 79, 83–4, 93; classrooms
    19, 49–50, 53; engaging 86; practical
    workshop sessions 50, 54, 68; sharing
    of ideas 50; students 37; teaching
    situations 48
Facebook 2, 38, 84, 94
faculty 1–3, 7–10, 13–14, 16, 19–23,
    68–9, 75, 81–2, 87–92, 94–100; and
    children 16; main ITE 59, 99; primary
    87; university ITE 5, 8, 24–6, 29–30,
    34–5, 37–8, 76–8, 80–1, 94–5, 98–9
freedom rides 62
Fullan, M. 1–2, 29–30
funding 21–4, 39, 96

game-based learning 2, 23
games 2, 5–6, 18, 23, 38, 52, 55, 64,
    87, 89–90; digital-technology 1;
    structured educational 15; and virtual
    worlds 87

Garrison, D. R. 19
Gibson, J. 17
Gill, L. 33–4
Gillen, J. 39
Glass, G. V. 1, 4
Google Cardboard 14
Google Earth 14
Google Sketch Up 14
graphics 19, 77, 95
Gregory, S. 5–6, 13, 23, 35–7
Gulbahar, Y. 4, 33–4

Hargreaves, A. 1–2
HCI 17; *see also* human computer
    interface; human computer interface;
    human computer interface design
Hedberg, J. 24, 32, 39
Heilig, M. 14
higher education 6, 10, 13, 16, 20, 24,
    33, 35; circles 7; faculties 21;
    institutions 6, 15; sector 7; studies
    46; users 22
Hirst, Damien 52
human computer interface 17

Initial Teacher Education 2, 4–5, 8–9,
    24–5, 33, 35, 46, 48–50, 99
innovation 1–3, 31, 52, 78, 91, 100; in
    education 1, 91; technologies 1, 3,
    10, 29, 31, 78, 88, 92, 95, 98
integration 3, 5, 20, 24–5, 75, 89–91,
    95, 98, 100; classroom 4; technology
    33, 88; of virtual worlds in teaching
    36, 88, 95
interactive technologies 35
ITE 2, 4–5, 8–9, 24–5, 33, 35, 46,
    48–50, 99; faculty and students 20,
    25, 33, 54, 75–7, 79, 82, 90–2, 98–9;
    faculty design 75; faculty reflection
    87; faculty training 81, 95; practising
    teachers 33; programmes 4, 9–10,
    24, 33–5, 45, 73, 97–8; students 5,
    24–6, 33–8, 45, 59, 61, 63, 82, 85,
    98–100; teacher programmes 5, 24,
    37; and technology students 24, 34;
    see also Initial Teacher Education

Jacka, L. 39, 95
Jacobson, L. 15
JISC 21; *see also* Joint Information
    Systems Committee

Johnson, C. W. 2, 39
Joint Information Systems Committee
    21

K-6 16, 59–60, 67, 69, 98; classrooms
    60, 69; education 59, 98; students 59
K-12: children 99; classrooms 32, 39,
    64, 74, 76, 79–80, 84, 98; education
    82, 87, 92, 94, 100; schools 38, 97;
    students 38, 75, 80; teachers 1, 26,
    29, 38, 88, 99
Kay, R. H. 24, 33–4
Kelton, A. 21
Kirriemuir, J. 21, 35
knowledge 3–5, 18, 26, 34–5, 52, 54,
    66–7, 88, 94; basic 96; content 25;
    pedagogical 25; technical 16;
    technological 25
Korea National University of Education
    36

labs 49–50
leadership role 96–7
learning 1–3, 5–6, 18–21, 23–4, 29–32,
    40, 73–6, 85–7, 94–5, 99–100;
    activities 4, 16, 20–1, 23, 47, 74, 94;
    experience 17, 19–20, 32, 52, 68–9,
    71, 74–5, 87, 89; game-based 2, 23;
    in higher education 16, 20; resources
    9, 47, 60; scenarios 16; spaces 6, 22,
    60, 94; tasks 18; technologies 9;
    theories 29; tools 54, 82; and virtual
    worlds 18, 20
learning environments 7, 30–1; adult
    16; controlled 86; positive 87
learning management systems 8, 14,
    18, 70, 79
lecture theatres 47, 49
Lee, M. J. W. 6, 18, 23, 37
LMS 8, 14, 18, 70, 79; *see also*
    learning management system
Lowendahl, J. M. 7

Machinimas (videos produced using
    screen-recording software) 58
management 23, 77, 95–6
Maraunchak, A. 7, 25
Masters, Y. 36
Mayo, N. B. 33–4
media 6, 16, 20, 31, 96; academic 38;
    digital 30; mass 5

medium 38, 96–7; complex visual 20;
    immersive 5; scale 96–7
Messinger, P. 35
micro-computers 31
Miller, A. 23, 76
mind-sets 80–1
mobile phones 31, 33, 96
Modanville PS 39
models 18, 20, 30, 32, 54, 94, 96, 98;
    extended 82; implementing new 1;
    partnering pedagogy 30; in second
    life 54; of teaching 20; traditional
    39–40, 100; transferable 54
MOOCs 1
Moodle 14
Moschini, E. 35
Moshi Monsters 15
motivations 76, 88, 91–2, 99; extrinsic
    4, 68, 76–7, 98; intrinsic 18; primary
    88
motivators 54, 98
music students 85

nature 1, 3–4, 15, 35, 85–6, 93;
    addictive 80; conservative 4;
    immersive 78; persistent 58; personal
    72; political 90
networks 8, 16, 80, 97; collaborative
    97; peer 48; persistent 13
New Media 9
New Media Consortium's Horizon
    Report 6
New Zealand 23, 25
Newman, C. 23
non-virtual world setting 72, 92
novices in virtual worlds 57, 87
Nussbaum, M. 3

objects 13, 16–18, 22, 45, 47, 56–8, 60,
    62, 64; interactive 56; physical 6;
    pre-made 54, 56, 62; primitive 46;
    ready-made 8
Oculus Rift 14
Office for Learning and Teaching 36
OLT 36; *see also* Office for Learning
    and Teaching
on-campus 9, 14, 19, 37, 45; classes 52;
    computer labs 46, 49, 51, 55, 69;
    facilities 37; lectures 55, 63; space 47;
    tutorials 36, 63, 69; workshops 47
online courses 32

online games 84
online interactions 20, 86
OpenSim 5–6, 16, 39; architecture 17; creators 17; environment 6, 16–17, 39, 96; users 17
Ottenbreit-Leftwich, A. 4, 31, 34

Painter, S. 34
parents 1–2, 15, 70–2; and the attraction of consents 15; and students 2; and the wider community 71
Parlett, M. 76
part-time jobs 76
part-time students 76
pedagogical 21–2, 34; choices 64; implications 75; practices 40; processes 25; shifts 35; transformation 34
pedagogical knowledge 25
pedagogy 3–4, 9–10, 18, 20, 22, 24–5, 87, 89–90, 94–6, 98–100; digital 5; implementing 25; innovative 33, 83, 95; and learning design 95; sound 6; student-centred 33; traditional 32, 83
perceptions 21–4, 66, 68, 72, 75–6, 79–80, 82, 84–6, 92–4; individual's 76; initial 94, 99; of ITE faculty and students 79; negative 81, 99; positive 73; pre-existing 94, 99; of virtual worlds for education 66, 82
phases 33, 82–4, 87, 98; planning 58; producing 58; of realization model 82
platforms 5–6, 16, 65, 96; e-learning 7; ideal 16; mature 8; virtual world 6, 16, 22
PlayStation 64
PowerPoint 47, 88
pre-realization phase 82–3, 87
Prensky, M. 30
Prestridge, S. 4
Primtings Museum 52
problem solving 36, 56, 87, 93
processing speeds 95
professional development services 96
professional development staff 96
programmes 8, 34, 66, 86; degree 9; distance-learning 7; inform ITE 100; pilot 39; teaching 4
publicity 8, 15, 100; mainstream 8; negative 15; positive 100

Radicati, S. 33
Raffaghelli, J. 34
rainwater tanks 55–6
RAM 23; *see also* random access memory
Ramsay, H. 22–3
random access memory 23
real teaching and learning 80
real time and space 85
recommendations 95–7, 100; and examples 100; made to assist the integration of virtual worlds in teaching and learning 95
reimagining phases 83, 87
representations 13, 94; enhanced spatial knowledge 18; graphical 5, 13–14; multimodal 51
research 8–10, 23–6, 37, 39, 76, 78, 82, 84, 90, 98–100; academic 90; data 99; information technology 6; in ITE 8; longitudinal 25; projects 34–6, 39, 62, 87, 98; sites 9; in virtual worlds 87
resources 4, 17–18, 37–8, 45, 51, 54–5, 59–60, 67–70, 97, 99; educational 59, 90; electronic 60; multimedia 20
responses 10, 13, 16, 52, 55, 66–8, 70, 72–3, 80–2, 94–5; emotional 78; evaluating 100; personal 84; positive 72; to virtual worlds 10, 67
role-playing 9, 36–7, 69–72; activities 19, 37; conversations 73; enabled real time 37; professional experience 37; scenarios 69–70, 86; situations 71

Savin-Baden, M. 20
Schome project 38–9
school students 37, 59, 62
schools 1–4, 9, 15, 17, 29–30, 35, 39–40, 93, 95, 97; elementary 46; meshing with homes 39; primary 60; secondary 9, 35, 46, 50; websites 39
science and technology education 9
Science and Technology Education 9
screen shots 51, 60, 64
Second Life 5–8, 16, 21–3, 35–7, 46–7, 53–6, 58–60, 62–4, 69–73, 78–80; accessing 39, 72–3; for education 16; and games on PlayStation and Wii 64; and information 59; and OpenSim 5, 14; preferred by some students 64; and Sim-on-a-Stick

(SoaS) 17, 39, 59–60, 62–4, 80, 86, 97, 99; for teaching and learning 36; teen grid 16

Selwyn, N. 75, 89–90

Sensorama 14

sessions 89, 97; mandatory tutorial 46; two-hour 58; unlimited informal 46

Sharpe, R. 31

Siemens, G. 29

Sim-on-a-Stick (SoaS) 17, 39, 59–60, 62–4, 80, 86, 97, 99

simulation 14, 18–19, 23, 47–8, 58, 61–2, 70; complex 60; effective 62; included 55; resources 8; virtual 23

skills 4, 24–5, 60, 63, 72–3, 75–6, 79, 87–90, 97, 99; basic 4, 47; collaboration 92; professional 37; social 79, 83–4, 86, 93; in virtual worlds 97

society 1, 3, 33, 39, 90–1; and digital literacy 90; networked 2

software 24, 34, 58

solar panels 54–7

space 5, 8, 10, 14–16, 18–20, 45–6, 49, 62–4, 85–6, 88–9; authentic 89; complete 9; designed 49; educational 19; immersive 25, 56; individual 17; introductory 47; open 55; and organizations 46; predesigned 59; shared 13, 18; student-centred 45; studio 64; traditional 40; virtual 40

Sploland 64

staff 70, 98; information technology 96; members 70

stakeholders 1, 3, 29, 90, 99

Stefanelli, C. 7, 25

student-faculty, ratio 52

student feedback 47, 68, 81

students 1–2, 5, 7–10, 19–23, 25, 29–30, 32–6, 45–60, 62–90, 92–100; interacting with the virtual world space 45; introduced to virtual worlds 35; in second life 58

Sumara, D. 10, 30

support 2–4, 21–3, 25–6, 31, 33, 45–6, 68, 77–9, 95–7, 99; for faculty and students 99; financial 17; higher level of 77; and introduction of the virtual worlds 95, 99; and level of technology 95

sustainability 7, 54–6; of building

practices 55; of design projects 9, 54–6, 60

Sutherland, I. 14

The Sword of Damocles 14

syllabus 36, 48, 51–2, 85–6; of creative arts 36; and proposed outcomes 86

tanks 55–6

teachers 1–5, 17, 19, 29–32, 37–40, 45, 51–3, 76–8, 80–1, 86–7; capacity of 3; flexibility of 100; individual 34; role of 30

teaching 1–4, 7–10, 16–17, 19–21, 23–5, 29–31, 34–6, 76, 82, 95; 21st-century 31; designated 9; developing virtual world 9; face-to-face 77; and learning affordances of virtual worlds 20; practice 36–7, 45, 51, 58, 74, 93, 98, 100; skill-based 58; spaces 22

Teaching the Teachers for the Future 25

technical knowledge 16

technical skills 70, 79, 83–4, 93, 96

technical support 16, 24, 88, 94

technological innovation 20, 32, 75

technological knowledge 25

technology 1–5, 17–18, 20, 23–6, 30–5, 37, 72–80, 82–6, 88–91, 93–5; computer 34; consumer-level 15; digital 26, 90; disruptive 31–2; emerging 3, 94; hardware 34, 78; integrating 3–4, 34; networked 2, 29; new 3, 7–9, 15, 25–6, 29, 75, 81, 89–90; role of 20; students 24, 34, 39; training 31; units 57, 60; of virtual worlds 20

Teen Second Life 39

text 19–20, 47, 55, 71, 93; and chat rooms 19, 71; and images 47

TFF project 25

Thomas, D. 20, 29–30

Tomlinson, Ray 33

tools 30, 32, 58, 66, 69, 78, 86, 89, 100; educational 17–18, 86; social networking 2; supplemental teaching 31

TPCK 25; *see also* technological pedagogical content knowledge

TTF 25; *see also* Teaching the Teachers for the Future

tutorials 9, 47–50, 55–6, 63, 79, 83, 89, 99; face-to-face 46, 69; regular 59; in second life 63; two-hour 9
tutors 7, 9, 21, 46, 53, 67, 99
Twining, P. 34–5, 39
Twitter 2, 38
Tyalla PS 39
Tynan, B. 6, 23, 36

universities 2–4, 7–9, 34–5, 37–8, 53–5, 58, 60, 67, 95–6, 98; and assignments using virtual worlds 73; and learning management systems 8; regional 9, 100
university campuses 8, 40, 77
university island 79–80
university management 8, 78, 95
university programmes 95
university settings 80
USB flash drives 17, 64
Utopia Island 52

Van Gogh 51
videos 19, 58, 70, 82
virtual campuses 7–8
virtual field trips 9, 51
virtual learning environments 6–7, 14, 16, 18–19
virtual reality 6, 14–15
virtual worlds 1–10, 13–26, 29, 35–40, 45–60, 62–4, 66–74, 76–100; acceptance in education 83; access to 21, 39; across platforms 6, 16, 22; activities 9, 88, 94; applications 13, 96; building skills 62; capacity for 21, 100; challenges 24; defined 13; disadvantages of 23; for educational purposes 87; and the environment 55, 94, 96–8; future iterations of the use of 67–8, 71, 81, 84–7, 94; in higher education 5–8, 13, 19–21, 23–4, 35, 64, 66, 70, 82, 98; integration in teaching and learning 36, 88, 95; to ITE faculty and students 92; in ITE programmes 35; in K-6 education 59, 98; in K-12 education 38, 92, 94, 97; networked social 17; perceptions of 82, 99; potential 25; of Second Life and Sim-on-a-Stick 99; and skills in workshops 97; in teaching 95; in university programmes 95
Virtual Worlds Working Group 13–14, 35
visual arts 45–6, 73, 85; and classrooms 85; curriculum 54; and education 36, 54; and students 46, 48–50, 52, 54, 56, 85; syllabus 48, 52
VLEs 6–7, 14, 16, 18–19; *see also* virtual learning environments
VR 6, 14–15; *see also* virtual reality
Vrasidas, C. 4
VWWG 13–14, 35; *see also* Australia and New Zealand Virtual Worlds Working Group

Wang, Y. M. 4–5
Warburton, S. 13, 19, 21, 35
Wasson, B. 26
websites 59, 70, 78, 82
Wenger, E. 19
Williams, M. 4
workshops 54–5, 59, 67, 69, 89, 97; and conferences 60; individualized group 70; one-to-one 63; in Second Life 89
World of Warcraft 38
World War I 64
Wright, Frank Lloyd 51

Xbox 14

Yammer 2
YouTube 71, 78
Yun, S. 36

Zagami, J. 36

Printed in the United States
by Baker & Taylor Publisher Services

Printed in the United States
by Baker & Taylor Publisher Services